W9-AYA-782

–LLEWELLYN'S–

2023

HERBAL
ALMANAC

Cover Designer: Kevin R. Brown
Editor: Lauryn Heineman

Interior Art: © Melani Huggins
Illustrations on pages 76, 272–74
by Llewellyn Art Department

You can order annuals and books from *New Worlds*,
Llewellyn's catalog. To request a free copy, call 1-877-
NEW WRLD toll-free or visit www.llewellyn.com.

ISBN: 978-0-7387-6393-4
Llewellyn Worldwide Ltd.
2143 Wooddale Drive
Woodbury, MN 55125-2989

Printed in the United States of America

Contents

DIY and Crafts

Plant Profiles

Gardening Resources

Introduction to
Llewellyn's Herbal Almanac

Holistic care for the mind, body, and soul starts in the garden. While adapting to the new normal, people around the world have sought out sustainable lifestyles and made greener choices, asking how to grow and preserve organic food for their family or how to forage for a nutritious bounty in their own neighborhood. Growing herbs enriches the soul, and using them in home-cooked meals, remedies, and crafts is clean, healthy, and just plain delicious.

There is no better time to grow, use, and eat herbs than now, and we hope you'll find inspiration for your own healthy life in this book. With sage advice appealing to novice gardeners and experienced herbalists alike, our experts tap into the practical and historical aspects of herbal knowledge—using herbs to help you connect with the earth, enhance your culinary creations, and heal your body and mind.

In addition to the twenty-two articles written by Master Gardeners, professors, homesteaders, and community herbalists, this book offers reference materials tailored specifically for successful growing and gathering. Use this book to log important dates, plot this year's garden, practice companion planting, garden by the moon, find a helpful herbal remedy, and keep track of goals and chores.

Reclaiming our connection to Mother Earth in our own backyards can bring us harmony and balance—and a delicious, healthy harvest. May your garden grow tall and your dishes taste divine!

Note: The old-fashioned remedies in this book are historical references used for teaching purposes only. The recipes are not for commercial use or profit. The contents are not meant to diagnose, treat, prescribe, or substitute consultation with a licensed health-care professional. Herbs, whether used internally or externally, should be introduced in small amounts to allow the body to adjust and to detect possible allergies. Please consult a standard reference source or an expert herbalist to learn more about the possible effects of certain herbs. You must take care not to replace regular medical treatment with the use of herbs. Herbal treatment is intended primarily to complement modern health care. Always seek professional help if you suffer from illness. Also, take care to read all warning labels before taking any herbs or starting on an extended herbal regimen. Always consult medical and herbal professionals before beginning any sort of medical treatment—this is particularly true for pregnant women. Herbs are powerful things; be sure you are using that power to achieve balance.

Growing
and
Gathering

Not Your Average Flower Garden

⤙ Melissa Tipton ⤚

Do you know what takes my breath away every time, without fail? That first springtime hike here in Missouri when the woodland flowers finally make an appearance, en masse, and the forest floor is blanketed in tiny colored stars. What a sight! And it's made all the more precious by how ephemeral it is. Before long, the woods are overtaken by a sea of unbroken greenery. In my own garden, I feel downright spoiled that I get to experience the beauty of flowers month after glorious month. In addition to more mainstream lovelies like asters, petunias, and zinnias, I like to include a cast of unconventional characters, inviting visitors (and myself) to lean in, slow down,

and stop and smell the bat flower. Let's take a peek at some of my favorites.

Toothache Plant (*Spilanthes*)

Make your flower bed pull double duty by mass planting the toothache plant along its border. These compact yellow buds, shaped like mini beehives, impart a gentle numbing sensation when chewed, effective even with dried flowers or prepared tinctures. I especially like the bull's-eye variety, with its golden-yellow flowers sporting rust-red centers. Not to mention, the toothache plant has such fun names: buzz button, electric daisy, and tingflower, to name just a few!

In addition to soothing toothaches, it has many other folk medicine uses, which include antimalarial, antifungal, and antibacterial applications. It can be used in treating tuberculosis and even snake bites (granted, these are things that, hopefully, you will never encounter), and the flowers have also demonstrated lipase-inhibitor properties, suggesting its relevance in controlling obesity. Not too shabby for such an unassuming little flower.

Gomphrena

The first time I planted gomphrena (the 'Strawberry Fields' variety), I was surprised at the spiky, papery feel of the living flowers, which were more like tiny pine cones than tender blossoms. This feature makes them well suited to flower arrangements, because they last an extraordinarily long time. You can use them in craft projects and dried flower displays too, and I love leaving them in my garden until fall, enjoying their bright pops of color outdoors, before harvesting them and weaving them into wreaths and other indoor projects for year-round visuals.

Gomphrena brings its striking, unusual blooms to sun-blazed, poor-soil spots where more tender plants would wilt and fade.

A relative of amaranth, gomphrena can be found in vivid red and rich orange varieties, as well as seed mixes with beautiful white, pale lavender, and deep magenta blooms, which are equally pretty in gardens or containers. And if, like mine, your garden has a few areas with less-than-amazing soil and blazing sun, you'll love how hardy these flowers are in conditions that might leave other plants wilted and unhappy.

Chinese Wool Flower
(*Celosia argentea* var. *childsii*)

These showy blooms do justice to their name, appearing more textile than plant with their fuzzy, bright-colored blossoms that are long-lasting and hardy. (I've had flowers stick it out past the first frost in some years.) The leaves also deliver a powerful nutritional punch with high levels of vitamin A and calcium, and they're easy to incorporate into recipes as a spinach substitute.

This celosia variety was introduced to the US in the early 1900s by the John Lewis Childs Seed Company, the first mail-order seed business in the States. (So I guess I know whom to thank for one of my favorite parts of gardening: pulling out all of my colorful seed catalogs over the winter and fantasizing about how epic next year's garden will be!) Despite its initial popularity, by the 1960s, Chinese wool flower became much harder to find, until it was entirely unavailable in the US. Jere Gettle of Baker Creek Heirloom Seeds was able to source a single pack of seeds from a Japanese supplier and then harvest seeds from his own plants, and now, happily, they're readily available once again.

Pink Dandelion (*Taraxacum pseudoroseum*)

In the woods near my house, purple and white violets can be found in abundance, but there are only two small patches where, if I'm lucky, I'll see a handful of delicate yellow violets in the spring. What, you might be asking, does this have to do with pink dandelions? Well, I've always found delight in uncommon variants of common things, and the pink dandelion definitely fits that bill.

The blooms feature the sunny yellow you'd expect at the center, but it's ringed by a pale cotton-candy pink. They're a great source of nectar for pollinators, such as butterflies and honeybees, and for us humans, they're a rich source of vitamin A, calcium, and other minerals. Like their yellow counterparts, the flowers, leaves, and roots are edible, and if you've ever made dandelion wine, how can you resist the temptation to make the pink-blossomed variety?

Rose Red Soba (*Fagopyrum esculentum*)

A version of the wild Himalayan pink buckwheat, harvested from the mountains and domesticated by Akio Ujihara, professor emeritus of Japan's Shinshu University, this gorgeous plant produces abundant sprays of pink blooms, attracting beneficial pollinators in droves. Since its domestication in the 1980s, many Japanese farmers have begun using it as a cover crop, and the fields of dazzling pink blossoms are so stunning, they've become a pit stop for tourists and pollinators alike.

Rose red soba can be used like common buckwheat, which in Japan includes brewing it into tea, grinding the seeds into a nutritious flour for noodles and cookies, and sprouting the seeds for microgreens. And research by Shinshu University showed that honey made from bees who fed on the rose-red variety was nearly 100 times higher in antioxidant effects than regular honey. And if *that* doesn't have you excited to add it to your garden, it's also deer-resistant, so no more going out to water your lovely plants in the morning, only to find they've been cropped into oblivion by voracious herbivores.

Honeywort (*Cerinthe major* 'Purpurascens')

Another pollinator superstar, these subtle, drooping blooms remind me of muted peacocks' tails with their indigo-purple petals. A relative of borage (another favorite in my garden, because the bees can't get enough of it), honeywort is native to the Mediterranean, and the ancient Greeks once believed it to be the source of the honeybee's wax.

I like mixing honeywort in with other, showier flowers and situating it near paths, as the blooms are best appreciated at close range. It's always fun to watch someone lean in to admire a more ostentatious neighbor before noticing honeywort's pretty purple bells, like they've stumbled onto a secret: "Oh! Look at those!" You can deadhead for longer blooms, and if you live in a milder climate, the plant will readily reseed. Where I live, I've had more success collecting the seeds and saving them for planting the following year. You can look for the seeds beneath the plant or cut off a blooming branch and put it in a paper bag to catch the seeds when they burst free.

Hopi Black Dye Sunflower
(a variety of *Helianthus annuus*)

Known as *Tceqa' Qu' Si* in Hopi, these tall plants yield an abundance of edible seeds and a lovely dye that ranges from a grayish lavender to a deeper velvety black, which is traditionally used in Hopi basketmaking as well as wool and cotton dying. Eat the seeds (or let the birds and squirrels go to town on them) and collect the hulls for dye making.

If you prefer a darker pigment, watch as the seeds first sprout and selectively thin them, leaving the ones with darker leaves (cotyledons, if you're feeling fancy), as those tend to produce a more richly hued dye. And for a beautiful and nutritious companion, you might add Hopi red dye amaranth to your garden as well.

Purple Stardust Iceplant
(*Delosperma floribundum*)

These delicate-looking flowers are hardier than they appear, and they readily form perennial ground cover mats in drier soils. I've always thought they looked a little undersea and anemone-like, in a beautifully alien way. If you really want an eye-catching mix, combine the purple stardust with the aptly named 'Fire Spinner' variety for a blanket of popping color.

I recently learned that iceplant is edible, and it can be eaten raw or cooked. I've added it to salads, to which it gives a mildly salty-sour crispiness, but I've also seen it used cooked as a spinach substitute. Another variety, the succulent iceplant, has leaves that, in addition to being edible, can be crushed to create a natural, soap-like lather (making it an interesting companion to the luffa gourd, which we'll talk about shortly!).

Painted Tongue Flower (*Salpiglossis sinuata*)

At first glance, you might mistake these for petunias with their frilly, streaked blooms. There are a few different varieties, and I'd be hard-pressed to pick a favorite—they're all so lovely! 'Grandiflora Mix' boasts pretty yellow, pinkish reds, and light purples, but you can also find a deep indigo 'Kew Blue', the delightfully goth magenta 'Black Trumpet', and the lavender-yellow contrast 'Royale Mixed.'

Salpiglossis, also known as the painted tongue flower, is a pretty addition to cut flower arrangements, and it will some-times put out a late-season burst of blooms, a last hurrah be-fore colder autumn temperatures set in. In my area, it didn't do well in a full-sun spot, but once I situated it in a place where it could cool off in the partial afternoon shade, it flourished and is now one of my garden favorites.

Luffa Gourd (*Luffa aegyptiaca*)

This delightfully bizarre plant is a vining gourd that produces a tasty, okra-like fruit related to the cucumber when harvested young. But if you leave the fruit to mature and completely dry out, peel off the skin, and remove the seeds, you now have yourself a loofah sponge. It's truly weird and wonderful to produce something from your very own garden that, in my experience at least, is typically only encountered in the aisles of Bed Bath & Beyond!

If you don't have a lot of space, the plant can be grown vertically. I've seen these grown with other vining plants on a walkway pergola, and the experience of walking under the leafy shade, skinny gourds dangling from above with their lemon-yellow, wrinkly blossoms catching the sunlight, was downright magical.

'Split Second' Morning Glory
(*Ipomoea purpurea*)

This was the first morning glory variety I had ever seen without the classic trumpet-shaped blooms. 'Split Second' has a frilly, tissue-paper cluster of pretty pink-and-white blossoms that look more like a peony than a morning glory, and the vines are vigorous climbers. The plants will often reseed, and in my area, which can get rather scorching in the heat of the day, they were happiest in a spot with afternoon shade. Once established, they were incredibly low-fuss, prolific bloomers. You can also plant them in containers and train them onto trellises or rods to corral them within a chosen area.

Big Leaf Tong Ho
(*Glebionis coronarium*)

Also known as chop suey greens, garland chrysanthemum, and edible chrysanthemum, this is another plant that boasts pretty blooms *and* nutritious greens. The flowers are reminiscent of daisies (which makes sense, given that they're in the daisy family) and have bright yellow centers blending into white or pale yellow edges. And while the greens, which are crunchy and meaty when cooked, are tasty and delicious, you can also eat the large flowers breaded in tempura, steeped as a tea, or sprinkled on salad as a gorgeous edible garnish.

Bat Flower (*Tacca chantrieri*)

This one could easily earn its place on our list by name alone, but the bat flower's bizarre blooms don't disappoint either. There are different species of *Tacca*, but the *chantrieri* has purplish-black flowers with two bracts (these are leaves that look like flower petals) shaped like bats' wings. But perhaps the most eye-catching feature is the long, whiskery bracteoles that hang down from the flowers, reaching lengths of up to ten inches.

In my area, it's easier to grow the bat flower in containers because it doesn't fare well in chilly weather, and this makes it easy for me to bring it indoors, where it enjoys bright, indirect light, but if you live in warmer climes, you can situate it in a shady spot. It likes moist soil, so I keep potted bat flowers in a saucer of water so I don't have to fuss with it as often. And if you feed it with orchid fertilizer, it will love you for life. Unlike many of the other flowers on this list, I wouldn't recommend using bat flower in cutting arrangements; it just doesn't last, and it's too depressing to see these beautiful blooms decline rapidly in vases.

Lady's Slipper Orchids (*Cypripedium*)

I was a little hesitant to include this beautiful plant because gardeners must do their due diligence to ensure they're not buying wild-harvested specimens, which threatens the stability of native plant populations. Generally, the price point will tip you off. If the plant is less than thirty dollars, chances are it's wild-harvested and should be avoided. Like most orchids, lady's slippers can be a little finicky, so it pays to do a little homework before adopting one to ensure you have the proper setup. Generally, moist, well-drained, and slightly acidic soil keeps them satisfied.

Lady's slippers have something of the exotic about them with their strange-looking parts and appendages, a feature they share with the rest of the orchid family. The "slipper" portion of the flower invites insects inside, and by the time they find the rear exit, they've unwittingly transferred pollen to the plant's stigma. These orchids hold a special place in my heart because of a childhood card game I adored called *Goldenrod: A Game of Wild Flowers*. Every card had a little painting by Ruth Wheeler, and the orchid family was unquestionably my favorite, because the paintings were darker, moodier, and more mysterious than the rest.

———

If, like me, you enjoy weaving a bit of the unexpected into the ordinary, these unique plants will add color and unconventional charm—and in the case of the luffa gourd, bathing implements!—to your garden.

Where Do Honeybees Go?

≈ Kathy Martin ≈

I was just in my backyard visiting
my beehives. It's a beautiful late
September day here in New England.
The tree leaves are starting to turn red
at the edges, and already most of our
flowers have faded and gone to seed.
I have two beehives: a tall, strong one
with five stacked boxes and a weaker,
shorter one that I split from the big
one this spring. I've been keeping bees
for about six years now, and I usually keep one or two hives at a time.
My honeybees are active today, flying
about, zipping in and out of the hive.
They gather on the landing board and
mill about, doing their wiggle dances.
The returning foragers are covered
with pollen—a hint to where they
have been.

I always wonder where my honeybees are going. It's an unusual thing to raise an animal (well, an insect) for food (honey), but another to let them go loose all day into other people's yards and who knows where else to forage. To figure out where honeybees have been, I do this:

- Research the plants honeybees do and do not visit
- Check what's in bloom and look for large expanses of native flowers
- Look at the pollen colors inside the hive
- Check honey color and—my favorite—taste the honey flavor!

When honeybees are out, they are busy collecting two things from flowers: nectar and pollen. Nectar is a sugar-rich solution produced by flowers. It is the source of energy for bees, powering their wing muscles and allowing them to make heat for the honeybee colony during the winter. Honeybees process nectar to make honey. In a fascinating manner, the bees deposit regurgitated nectar into wax cells and fan it with their wings until it has a moisture content of about 18 percent, a level at which it will keep forever without spoiling. Then they cap the honey cell with wax so that it stays at that density. What an amazing thing honeybees do! Honeybees' other food source, pollen, provides everything else the bees need to thrive, including proteins, fats, and an assortment of micronutrients, vitamins, and minerals.

Since it is approaching winter now here in New England, I will soon open my hives and check to make sure to the bees have plenty of stored honey and pollen. These are the riches from their spring, summer, and fall foraging around my yard, around the neighborhood, and maybe even across and to the other side of town.

Plants Honeybees Do and Do Not Visit

Bees are attracted to plants that produce nectar and pollen. Some of the best flowers for honeybees have single flowers. In general, the single flower invests more energy in nectar production and less in petal formation. Hybrids with double flowers and large blooms generally are all show as far as a bee is concerned. Native plants reliably produce the nectar and pollen on which bees depend.

Bees' flower preferences also are due to the way they see the world. Honeybees have five eyes, specialized structures that see flowers differently than humans do. Honeybees can see UV light, unlike humans, but red looks black to a bee. Bees see the colors blue, purple, and yellow and find flowers in these colors the most appealing.

In the northern US, plants that are major sources of nectar for honeybees in the earliest spring, often when it is too cold for bees to fly, include native maples and willows. As the weather warms, honeybees visit dandelions and many varieties of clover. In summer, the foraging list expands, and major honeybee pollen sources in the Northeast include black locust, sumac, blackberries, raspberries, basswood, milkweed, fireweed, and smartweed. In the northern US in fall, honeybees love goldenrod, thistles, tansy, and many types of asters. In addition to these native plants, there are many garden plants that honeybees love. In my garden, honeybee favorites are catmint, holly, purple coneflower, black-eyed Susan, sedum, Joe Pye weed, liatris, mint, lavender, chives, hyssop, and basil.

Check What's in Bloom around You and Look for Large Expanses of Flowers

Fifty feet away from my beehives is a big pond and conservation land. I know my honeybees frequent the flowers at the edge of the pond in the spring and summer. I have often paddled around the pond in my kayak, sometimes with my dogs perched at the bow and binoculars in hand, to see where my bees are going. Plants at the edge of the pond include swamp maples, willows, azalea, blueberry, sweet pepper bush, button bush, goldenrod, and purple loosestrife. I've seen honeybees in each of these. I have also seen them in the white and yellow water lilies that float on the pond.

Older honeybees who have the strongest flight muscles are the ones who go out of the hive and gather honey and pollen.

One mile away from my hives, as the bee flies, is a field full of wild fall New England asters, lots of small white ones and even more of the larger purplish wood asters. The field is bright, beautiful, and noisy, covering an acre or so. My dogs and I went up close to look and found every type of bee—small wasps, little bumblebees, bigger bumblebees, and honeybees. I would guess there was at least one bee per square inch, so that's literally 10 million bees in that one acre! Most of the bees I saw there were native; I'd guess maybe 10 percent were honeybees. An average beehive is home to 30,000 honeybees, which means bees from 30 local honeybee hives could have been out there together gathering food in that one field! I would imagine some of my bees are out there.

Foraging honeybees are out and about for four hours a day, and each will visit about 1,200 flowers in that time. Wow! A lot of flowers. The foraging area around a beehive is typically two miles (3.2 kilometers), although bees have been observed foraging much further from their hive.

My honeybees are not world travelers like the migratory farmers' hives that follow harvests for pollination. Now those honeybees go places! They start the spring season in California pollinating almond trees, then some bees are transported to the cherry, plum, and avocado orchards in California or to the apple or cherry orchards in Washington State. In summertime, many beekeepers bring their hives east to pollinate alfalfa, sunflower, and clover fields in North and South Dakota. Others visit squashes in Texas, clementines and tangerines in Florida, cranberries in Wisconsin, and blueberries in Michigan and Maine. Along the East Coast, honeybees are moved around to pollinate apples, cherries, pumpkins, cranberries, and various vegetables. By November, the migratory bee colonies are moved south to warm areas to wait out the winter. Surprisingly, some beehives wait out the winter in temperature-controlled potato cellars in Idaho.

Pollen Color Can Tell You Where Your Honeybees Have Been

Many of us in my local beekeeping club talk about where our bees are going at different times of the year. Often, it's places where we don't see them. Many large trees are excellent sources of nutrition, and we don't necessarily see bees there. But what we can observe is the pollen they bring back to the hive. Honeybees store pollen in cells that are separate from the cells they put nectar into, and the pollen has a wide range of colors. I have seen collected pollen that is so dark it is almost black. It can also be brown, green, golden, orange, yellow, pale to deep yellow, and even light blue. You can find pollen color charts online. The North Carolina State Beekeepers Association has a nice chart showing the range of local pollen color at ncbeekeepers.org/resources/flowering-plants.

For pollen in my hive, I see the light yellow of willow, pale brown of red maple, and lime green of sugar maple first in the spring. Willow trees do not produce much nectar, but the bees love the pollen it produces. Then in May, crab apple pollen is a bit more greenish and wild cherry pollen is more golden. Dandelion pollen is a bright orange. In mid-summer, I can find golden pollen from sunflowers, sunburnt brown from clover, and sometimes a cell or two of yellowish white from jewelweed. In August, Joe Pye weed and Japanese knotweed pollen are dark, almost black. The sweet pepperbush that is so prolific around the pond in August has golden pollen. Late fall flowers, the ones I am seeing now, include goldenrod with its golden pollen and aster with reddish yellow pollen.

The colors of pollen from cultivated crops are also interesting to look for. Asparagus pollen is bright orange; onion is light olive; borage is blueish-gray; marigold is bright orange; cucumbers, melons, and pumpkins are bright yellow; basil is white; and sweet corn is yellowish white. My bees are not only next to a pond but also right next to my vegetable garden. The color palette of their pollen is amazing in the summer!

Honey Color and Taste Can Tell You Where Your Bees Have Been

The color and flavor of honey differs depending on the flowers the bees have collected it from. The National Honey Board says that "there are more than 300 unique types of honey available in the United States, each originating from a different floral source. Honey color ranges from nearly colorless to dark brown, and its flavor varies from delectably mild to distinctively bold, depending on where the honeybees buzzed. As a rule, light-colored honey is milder in taste and dark-colored honey is stronger." There are as many unique honeys as there are flowers that bees visit!

Varietal honey (honey produced from a primarily a single source of flower) is completely different from the mass-produced, blended honeys, in which individual flavors are lost. A nice table of honey varieties and their tastes and colors is listed on the food website the Nibble: thenibble.com/reviews /main/honey/types4.asp.

Maple honey is one of the earliest that my bees collect. It has a mild, light, and unique flavor. Clover honey is a classic that is yellow in color with a sweet, flowery mild taste. Blueberry honey is golden with a mild lemony aroma and a moderate fruity flavor. My sweet pepperbush honey is my favorite. It's golden yellow with a slight tinge of red. The flavor is sweet, herbal, and mellow with a hint of licorice and a slightly spicy aftertaste. In my hives, I always recognize the Japanese knotweed honey that the bees collect in late-August. It is dark and reddish in color with a rich flavor. Even though knotweed is a non-native, invasive plant in New England, it is nutritious for honeybees, and they love it.

In the late fall, my honeybees collect goldenrod honey, which is medium amber in color. My bees also collect lots of aster honey, which is lighter in color. Aster and goldenrod honey both bring a strong smell to the hive. Some beekeepers describe it as musty, sour, or yeasty and leave it in the hive for the bees to eat over the winter. However, I find that the hive aroma does not reflect the taste of the honey, and it has a pleasant, sweet herbal taste, with a hint of butterscotch.

Why Do We Want to Know Where Our Honeybees Go?

When my honeybees are out foraging, I'm curious about where they are going. It's good animal husbandry to keep track of them and be aware of problems they may encounter. Bees are at risk of many dangers now, especially colony collapse disorder, the sudden disappearance of a beehive's residents. Multiple factors are known to contribute to colony collapse: mites that carry diseases, pesticide use, long-distance transportation of colonies and migratory beekeeping practices, and limited floral resources. The most pressing threats to long-term bee survival have been shown to include climate change, habitat loss and fragmentation, invasive plants and bees, declining genetic diversity, pathogens spread by commercially managed bees, and pesticides. When I saw my bees foraging around our pond, I investigated the quality of the water and the ecosystem there. When I see my bees in local fields, I like to ask if pesticides are being used.

Looking into honeybee habitat issues also reminds us that honeybees are not the only type of bee in danger now. Challenges face honeybees and our native bees. There is an important difference between the two. Honeybees are someone's livestock. They are domestic insects and not a native species. In North America, four types of bumblebee are in decline, and one has recently become extinct. And there are many other types of bees that we know don't know much about. It appears that nearly fifty eastern North American bee species are in decline. But for sure, most things that we can do to support honeybees will also support natives. So, follow the bees, find out where they are going, and do what you can to help keep them healthy!

Resources

Jabr, Ferris. "The Mind-Boggling Math of Migratory Beekeeping." *Scientific American*, September 1, 2013. https://www.scientific american.com/article/migratory-beekeeping-mind-boggling -math/.

National Honey Board. "Honey Flavor and Color." Accessed January 28, 2022. https://honey.com/newsroom/presskit/honey-color -and-flavor.

The Nibble. "Honey Types, Page 4: Popular Honey Varietals." Last modified October 2012. https://www.thenibble.com/reviews /main/honey/types4.asp.

Pain, Stephanie. "The Whole Food Diet for Bees." *Knowable Magazine*, December 4, 2017. https://knowablemagazine.org/article /sustainability/2017/whole-food-diet-bees.

A Blue and Purple Herb Garden

❧ Suzanne Ress ❧

When considering what herbs to plant in a newly established garden, you might take into account the colors of their flowers. Herbal plants are those whose parts can be used for medicinal or culinary purposes. Common examples include the following:

Leaves, Fresh or Dried: Basil, parsley, oregano, savory, and rosemary

Seeds: Dill, caraway, fennel, and anise

Flower Pistils and Pollen: Saffron and fennel

Root or Bulb: Licorice, horseradish, ginger, and curcumin

The added bonus of almost all herbs and herb gardens is that they bloom, giving us a spiritual lift with their diverse and colorful flowers.

Consider the color of an herbal plant's flowers when selecting it and when deciding where in the garden to place it in relation to other herbs. Rather than a hodgepodge of yellow, white, orange, red, and blue, I think an all blue and purple flowering herb garden is inspirational.

Why blue and purple? Because these colors, apart from having a magical quality to them, can create an atmosphere of freedom, tranquility, and wisdom.

Blue, one of the three primary colors, is so mutable that it seems to be more a condition of light than a solid color. Think of all the various shades called "blue"—from the pale glowing electric blue of morning snow, to powder blue, to baby boy blue, cadet blue, cerulean, royal blue, Prussian blue, navy, and midnight blue, which is almost black. What does the palest skim milk white blue have in common with the deepest midnight sky blue? I think it is just a tone that isn't red or yellow! The variations in blue tone seem to me to be the widest. It is a boundless "color" and, in all of its mutations, gives me a feeling of freedom, expanse, imagination, and unlimited possibility.

The color purple, which is blue with red added, has less variation, from light and delicate mauve tones to lilac, lavender, and violet. While blue seems an endlessly spacious color, purple is the color of enchantment, dreams, spirituality, and wisdom.

We see blue as blue because, in the light spectrum visible to most humans, blue wavelengths are the shortest. These short wavelengths have a sedative effect on us that slows pulse rate and lowers blood pressure. Purple shades combine this shortest wavelength with the longest, red. Red wavelengths have the opposite effect on us: excitement, increased pulse. Purple is sort of like adding a shot of whiskey to your coffee—something unexpected happens.

Both blue and purple are associated with the sky, purple with the threshold times of dawn and dusk. The changing light throughout a day or season, including clouds and other weather conditions, has a great effect on colors we see in nature, particularly on blues and purples. A blue and purple flowering garden at dawn in July looks different from the same garden at midday or at dusk, in the month of May, in September, when the sky is dark with storm clouds, when a gentle rain is falling, or when the sky is clear and bright. Each of these changes in light can transform the appearance of a flowering blue and purple garden.

When deciding what to plant, keep in mind blooming seasons of each plant, height, and width, as well as the plant's particular needs for sun, shade, drainage, and type of soil. I have divided my list of blue and purple flowering herbs by flowering season. Be aware that many herbs will flower continuously for months, and, depending on what growing zone you live in, some may flower earlier or later than my list suggests.

Spring Purple-Flowering Plants
Violet (*Viola odorata*), Perennial
Violet spreads via stolons that root at the tips, and it prefers damp, shady places. Violet flowers can be eaten in salads or desserts, and the plant's leaves have antiseptic properties.

Lungwort (*Pulmonaria officinalis*), Perennial
Lungwort grows in shady places and prefers not to be crowded. About the size of lilies-of-the-valley, these odorless beauties

sport white-spotted lung-shaped leaves, and blue, purple, and pink flowers on the same plant. A decoction made from the whole plant is used as an expectorant.

Liverwort (*Hepatica nobilis*), Perennial
This plant spreads by rhizomes. Lovely green- and white-striped leaves stay green all year, with small light purple-blue flowers. Dried liverwort can be used to treat liver problems, but beware that the fresh herb and flower are toxic.

Periwinkle (*Vinca major*), Perennial
Periwinkle spreads by rooting shoots and stems. Its shiny deep green leaves remain green all year, and its purple-blue flowers can be removed and sucked at the base for a drop of sweet nectar. The leaves can be made into an astringent tea, good to lessen heavy menstruation or bleeding piles.

Honesty (*Lunaria annua*), Biennial
Honesty likes plenty of light and will grow in poor soil. These cheery, bright purple, daisy-high flowers transform into silvery discs that resemble coins in the fall. The plants are believed to attract good fortune. The leaves and the flowers can be added to salads, and the seeds inside the silver discs have a pungent taste and can be used like mustard seed.

Chives (*Allium schoenoprasum*), Perennial
Chives like full or partial sun. The young, tender greens are popular chopped and sprinkled on vegetables, but once they form flower buds, the greens become tough. The flower buds and flowers are light violet little globes and can be eaten on salads.

Spring Blue-Flowering Plants

Blue Flag Iris *(Iris versicolor)*, **Perennial**

This iris spreads through rhizomes and self-seeds, and it thrives in sunny places with rich, moist soil. The large blooms are bright deep blue. Iris is poisonous in all of its parts, but its root can be dried and ground to make orris root powder, a light, violet-scented fixative used in potpourri.

Blue Bugle (*Ajuga reptans*), **Perennial**

This low-growing ground cover has small stems of spiraling bright blue flowers. Its leaves can be used to help staunch bleeding. It is an early season attractant to butterflies, bees, and other pollinators.

Summer Purple-Flowering Plants

Devil's Bit (*Succisa pratensis*), **Perennial**

The devil's bit likes full sun and can stand drought conditions. It will flower all summer with light purple pincushion-shaped blossoms, one on each long stem (daisy-height). An infusion made from the flowers can help inflammatory conditions.

Lavender (*Lavandula angustifolia*), **Perennial**

This is one of my personal favorite herbal plants. Lavender blooms in early summer in various shades of purple and blue (depending on the variety) and can grow to about three feet high and wide. It loves full sun and well-draining soil. Lavender flowers can be used in marinades, sprinkled on poultry and pork before grilling, and also used in potpourri, teas, and infusions. The silvery-green needle-like foliage is excellent fresh or dried, strewn over meats or potatoes.

Rosemary (*Salvia rosmarinus*), Perennial

Sun-loving rosemary can withstand drought. Years ago, I planted a dozen little creeping rosemary plants on a walled-in, south-facing slanted rooftop. Ten years on, and the rosemary completely covers the roof and dangles down off the sides of the wall. It is in bloom on and off (mostly on) from April through October and is an excellent extra nectar source for my honeybees. Rosemary is one of the classic cooking herbs (*fines herbes*) and, additionally, has antiseptic properties.

Sage (*Salvia officinalis*), Perennial

This is another silvery-leaved classic kitchen herb. Its leaves can be used fresh or dried but become more pungent when dried. Sage is drought tolerant and can thrive in poor soil. It blossoms in mid-summer with lovely bluish-purple flowers. Sage comes in many varieties. It has antibacterial qualities, can be made into an infusion, and can be used to make a yellow dye. The dried leaves are also great for smoke cleansing.

Pennyroyal (*Mentha pulegium*), Perennial

Preferring moist soil and partial sun, pennyroyal grows to about a foot in height and produces pale purple tufted flowers. Its leaves have long been used as a remedy for flatulence and abdominal pains, but the plant itself should not be boiled, and no parts of it are safe for pregnant women.

Hyssop (*Hyssopus officinalis*), Perennial

Drought tolerant and preferring partial sun, hyssop is one of the world's oldest known cultivated herbs and one of the bitter herbs. Its leaves can be used to flavor soups and stews or added to homemade liquors. Its long stems full of small deep purple flowers bloom in mid to late summer. It is a great butterfly and bee attractant.

Lamb's Ears (*Stachys byzantina*), Perennial
Self-seeding and drought tolerant, lamb's ears is also called the woolly hedge nettle because of its soft silvery, furry foliage. The leaves can be used as poultices and have analgesic properties. Its lilac-colored little flowers grow in a whorled fashion around the furry silver stems in late summer.

Holy Thistle or Milk Thistle (*Silybum marianum*), Annual
Freely self-seeding, this is a large, unruly, thorny-leaved plant that produces big, light purple, thorn-rimmed thistle flowers in mid-summer. The greens and flower buds can be stripped of their thorns, boiled or steamed, and eaten, and they are full of flavonolignans, powerful compounds that protect the liver from toxins.

Russian Sage (*Salvia yangii,* syn. *Perovskia atriplicifolia*), Perennial
Russian sage has silvery-green lacy fronds with many long, delicate panicles of small light purple flowers that go on blooming from mid-summer into fall. The plant is drought tolerant and hardy. Its little flowers can be sprinkled on salads or crushed and used as a purple dye. The greens can be dried and smoked, as they contain thujone, a euphoriant. The whole plant repels insect pests.

Speedwell (*Veronica officinalis*), Perennial
Speedwell likes partial sun and spreads via creeping stems. Its flowers are deep purple and snapdragon shaped, and the whole full, pretty plant grows to about eight inches high. An

infusion of the dried leaves is used as an expectorant, good for speeding up the healing of colds, hence its common name.

Passionflower (*Passiflora incarnata*), Perennial
Passionflower likes partial sun or shade and moist, well-draining soil. Its beautiful lavender and purple tropical-looking blooms open on climbing vines. Passionflower extract, decoctions, and teas have a narcotic effect and are an effective sedative used to treat tension.

Mallow (*Malva sylvestris*), Self-Seeding Annual
Mallow grows in sun or partial shade in any soil. Its blooms are bright pinkish-purple, and the whole plant can be used dried or fresh for decoctions and teas, turning bright blue in hot water. The tea is good for helping clear up urinary tract infections and for intestinal irritation.

Summer Blue-Flowering Plants

Borage (*Borago officinalis*), Self-Seeding Annual
Borage prefers full or partial sun and will grow to about a foot and a half in height and only a little less wide. Borage flowers are shaped like stars, incredibly bright blue with deep purple or violet accents. The flowers can be strewn on salads or summer drinks and add a fresh cucumber-like flavor. The plant's large hairy greens are tasty, steamed and chopped, with olive oil.

Purple Coneflower (*Echinacea purpurea*), Perennial
Also self-seeding, the purple coneflower likes full or partial sun and well-drained, moist soil. The flowers will grow to almost two feet in height, daisy-like, each flower on a long stem, with attractive deep green foliage. The roots of the echinacea

contain the caffeic acid glycoside, which creates a reaction in human body cells that promotes healing.

Flax (*Linum usitatissimum*), Self-Seeding Annual
Flax likes full sun and is usually grown by the field-full, but it can also be a pretty addition to an herb garden, with its small bright blue flowers, each on a long slender stem. Once the flowers fade and dry, brown pods remain, and it is here you will find the linseeds. These are the source of linolenic acid, an omega-3 oil, and are tasty toasted on cereals and breads. Just don't eat the seeds before they are completely dried, as they may be toxic. If you don't collect the seed pods, the plants will freely self-seed.

Black Cumin (*Nigella sativa*), Self-Seeding Annual
This herbaceous plant's foliage is bright green and feathery and looks like a mist in which its heavenly blue flowers are suspended. It is a lovely, delicate-looking plant, unlike any other. *Nigella* likes full sun. Once its flowers dry up, it produces small black edible seeds called black cumin.

Autumn Purple-Flowering Plants
Saffron Crocus (*Crocus sativus*), Perennial
I've seen these growing wild in sunny fields, but more often they must be cultivated. They are light purple and resemble the spring crocus but have slimmer leaves and higher stamens, and, of course, the spring crocus does *not* produce saffron. Saffron crocus's flower pistils and pollen are what the precious spice saffron is. This can be used in small quantities to delicately flavor egg dishes, risottos, and pasta, but it can be toxic in excess. A saffron infusion can also help with menstrual pain.

Wild Aster (*Symphyotrichum patens*), Perennial

The wild aster grows in good soil in partial sun and is an important last-of-the-season flowering plant for honeybees. The flowers are a striking bright purple, and both flowers and leaves are edible, in moderation, in salads. The plant spreads via suckers, dies in the winter, and is reborn in the spring.

Chicory (*Cichorium intybus*), Perennial

This herb is drought-tolerant and prefers full sun. It blooms from late summer through autumn with all sky-blue petalled flowers on tough stems. The roots of chicory are dried and ground to make a caffeine-free coffee substitute. It aids digestion and is mildly laxative.

———

This is a brief listing of some of the useful and beautiful purple and blue flowering herbs—there are many more! Research, explore, and experiment to create your own transcendent garden of peace, freedom, and wisdom!

Resources

Atha, Anthony. *The Ultimate Herb Book*. London: Collins and Brown, 2001.

Kowalchik, Claire, and William H. Hylton, eds. *Rodale's Illustrated Encyclopedia of Herbs*. Emmaus, PA: Rodale Press, 1998.

Potterton, David, ed. *Culpeper's Color Herbal*. New York: Sterling Publishing, 2002.

Theroux, Alexander. *The Primary Colors: Three Essays*. New York: Henry Holt, 1994.

———. *The Secondary Colors: Three Essays*. New York: Henry Holt, 1996.

Victorian Houseplants

⤝ Natalie Zaman ⤝

I love a house that's full of living
things—people (of course), pets,
and plants. I'll skip the bugs, but
the occasional spider is okay. At
the moment, I can't have a pet, and
plants . . . it's a challenge. Forced air,
closely sited neighboring houses that
block the sun, and my hefty work
schedule don't make my home the
ideal place for raising plants—a familiar problem to many wannabe horticulturists since time immemorial.

Keeping houseplants dates back
to ancient times, but there are certain eras that speak to me—the 1970s,
when everyone was making macramé
plant holders, and the eighteenth and
nineteenth centuries, when explora-
tion and trade brought tropical plants

to un-tropical climes in Europe and America. I grew up in the 1970s and have a thing for macramé, along with many fond memories. My aunt Jo had a special love for spider plants (macramé and spider plants were pretty much made for each other) and propagated enough cuttings to make a whole colony of them to fill her tiny apartment.

As for Victoriana, I love that complex British-Euro-American culture that embraced death (there's nothing quite like Victorian mourn-abilia) and life all at the same time. Nineteenth-century folks loved plants, outdoors as well as in. If you were well-to-do, a conservatory filled with tropical plants made a novel setting for afternoon tea or a refuge when you just wanted to surround yourself with beauty. But not everyone could afford to build elaborate, decorative greenhouses—or even "Wardian cases," miniature dollhouse confections built to hold exotic succulents and cacti—but there was always the reliable *Aspidistra elatior*, or cast-iron plant, a hardy houseplant that could survive neglect, extreme shade, and drafty nooks.

Nineteenth-century folks kept houseplants for much the same reasons we do:

- Plants can help improve mental health. Consider the psychology of color; greenery naturally warms and brightens the dingiest of spaces. (Green is a combination of calming blue and positive yellow.) Being outdoors, especially on a gorgeous day, can improve the spirit. Bringing a bit of the outdoors inside can have a similar effect. In the 1920s, when she lived in a cold water flat in downtown Manhattan, my nonna (born in the nineteenth century) kept a snake plant, another practically indestructible houseplant. Her New York apartment had little light, and Nonna had little time to tend to it as she worked all day. My grandmother grew up in a green and rural part of southern Italy; I'm sure having the plant helped ease the transition to city life and perhaps brought memories of home.

- Plants may help improve air quality. As part of the natural process of photosynthesis, plants release oxygen during the day.

- Plants are practical. Houseplants exist for their own sake and provide the intangible benefits already described, but many also generate usable produce. Kitchen gardens have been an integral element of households of the past, but there are several varieties of plants that are simultaneously decorative and useful.

- Plants send messages—literally, for the nineteenth-century crowd. We're talking about an age when sentimentality was often expressed symbolically; every flower and leaf had levels of meaning determined by color, shape, and scent. An evergreen, ivy denoted a happy marriage. A nosegay of daisies was given for attachment and, of course, roses were given for love. What kind of love depended on the color: white for purity, yellow for friendship, and red for romantic love.

Before We Begin . . .

Looking to the past gave me hope that I, too, could have houseplants without killing them. I won't lie; trial, error, and casualties were part of the process. These are some things to keep in mind when building your indoor Victorian garden:

Start Small: My first mistake was to try to care for too many plants at once. Once I found that I was able to take care of one plant fairly well, I added another, and then another.

Start Easy: Why make things hard on yourself? There are plenty of plants cherished in the nineteenth century that are relatively easy to care for.

Be Observant: Watch for changes in your plants—they will show you when they need help. I know to water my philodendron when its leaves start to look a little droopy. Sometimes changing where a plant lives in your home can also make a difference if there is a problem.

Don't Be Discouraged: Sometimes a plant is going to die for any number of reasons. Before replacing it, do some detective work to find out why your plant did not survive. You may, indeed, be the cause of its demise. I've learned the hard way that overwatering is just as bad as being forgetful about watering plants. However, it's just as likely that there are things beyond your control. It may be that your space just does not have the right lighting or humidity to keep a certain plant alive. Just about every kind of environment can support some type of plant life. Any plant you can't grow, you can experience elsewhere—and sometimes this is an opportunity to experience some real Victorian-era conservatories firsthand. Some of my favorites are the Enid A. Haupt Garden in the New York Botanical Garden; the Conservatory at Longwood Gardens in Kennett Square, Pennsylvania; and the Orchid Range at Duke Farms in Hillsborough, New Jersey—and there is always the artwork of Edward Gorey, a twentieth-century artist with Victorian sensibilities.

The following are some easy peasy lemon squeezy Victorian houseplants. Okay, maybe not all the plants are "easy," but these are the varieties with which I've had luck . . . or at least experience.

The Fern

A Victorian houseplant that scents the air.

Why they loved it: Ferns are a quintessential Victorian houseplant (especially the Boston fern), with frothy fronds spilling out over pots or hanging baskets and giving that fashionable, tropical feel to a space. Scent is not the first thing that you might think of when it comes to ferns, but the truth is that many if not all varieties of fern have distinct scents (though the leaves may need to be crushed to release it). The leaves of the smallest member of the Boston fern family, the lemon button fern, give off a lovely citrus scent—who would have thought?

Why I love it: I'm with my Victorian forebears on ferns—no other plant is so lush. Confession: I've had better luck with ferns outdoors, planted directly into the ground, though I still haven't given up on indoor ferns yet.

Know before you grow: Ferns like humidity along with damp soil and filtered sunlight. In my house with its forced air, the humidity is a bit of a challenge, and I find myself misting my fern quite a bit. You may have better luck with this plant if your home has steam heat or if you live in an environment that has higher degrees of humidity. Another trick to upping the humidity in your space is to group plants together.

The Aloe

A Victorian houseplant that is medicinal.

Why they loved it: Wardian cases were a popular, though expensive, nineteenth-century item since their invention in 1820. These elaborate mini greenhouses, often kept on an equally elaborate stands, were jewel cases for rare plants. The succulent, tropical aloe was an ideal candidate for the Wardian case, where it could be kept safely out of cold temperatures even in the winter.

Why I love it: If spiders were Aunt Jo's favorite plants, I would have to say that the aloe comes in as a close second. Once again, a family memory makes this plant dear to me, as I remember my aunt snipping off a piece of aloe to rub on a scrapes, as it has medicinal properties. (Do not use any plant as medicine without first consulting with a health care professional!)

Know before you grow: Aloes like damp, not soaking, soil and lots of sun. Watch your aloe and it will tell you what it needs: drooping leaves means she needs more sun, while thin, curling leaves means more water is needed.

You can build your own mini Wardian case and do the planet a favor too. The next time you buy berries, save the plastic container (especially the large tall ones that hold strawberries). The holes in the bottom of these containers make for perfect drainage and ventilation, and the snap lids will help hold heat in. Once populated with plants, you can add dollhouse furniture, fish tank decorations (like a mini pagoda), or decorative stones or crystals to create a "scene" for your plants.

The Citrus

A Victorian houseplant that produces fruit.

Why they loved it: In England, the abolition of the glass tax in 1845, followed quickly by the invention of plate glass, lowered the barrier to entry for greenhousery and the like. One still had to have some means to possess a full greenhouse, but the growing season for the smallest of kitchen gardens increased with this development. In the British Isles, citrus fruit was imported; hothouse citrus trees made these fruits—sometimes given as gifts at Christmas—more readily available.

Why I love it: When my nonna was in the hospital for the last time, she'd eaten a grapefruit and, as was her way, kept one of the seeds and planted it in a Styrofoam cup. Eventually, the little seed sprouted into a tree that eventually became a houseplant—living outside during the summer months when the New Jersey weather was more citrus-tree friendly. She (the plant) is still with us but sadly never produced fruit.

Know before you grow: A grapefruit tree grown from seed takes at the very least three years to produce fruit. To be honest, we were just amazed that our tree has survived for so long—we didn't pursue trying to help her fruit; nutrients in the soil and proper pruning and pollination techniques all play a part. I'm content to have her as a living tribute to my nonna, but that said, it is entirely possible for a grapefruit, or any citrus fruit, grown from seed to produce fruit. Of course, you can also get a tree already producing fruit from a nursery. Light and warmth are key environmental elements for keeping citrus trees alive and happy, but getting them to fruit takes a bit of extra work. Heather Buckner's article "Growing Citrus Indoors: Create a Little Slice of Paradise" is a great primer for building an indoor citrus orchard (see references at the end of this article).

The Ivy

A Victorian plant that conveys a message.

Why they loved it: Climbing, clinging ivy marries whatever it embraces, making it a fitting symbol of constancy—who wouldn't want to live in an ivy-draped cottage, if only for that reason? Also loved as an indoor plant in the nineteenth century, ivy draped from hanging baskets along with ferns. It could serve, with the proper training, to outline anything from a piece of furniture to a fireplace. And of course, along with holly, ivy was used liberally in Yuletide decorating.

Why I love it: I'd always dreamed of a house overgrown with English ivy—a dream made into reality, but it took a long time; when first planted, ivies are slow growers, but when they hit about year three, things speed up and they start to climb. (Look closely at ivy vines and you'll see little roots on them—this helps them cling to vertical surfaces!)

Know before you grow: Ivy is indeed a shade-loving plant—but it still needs bright light. According to several sources, including my go-to resource, Gardening Know How, indoor ivies do best with bright light and rich soil that is on the dry side.

———

My houseplants brighten my space, but they also have roots in my past, seeds of memories that sprout to the surface of the present whenever I look at and care for them. When adding Victorian houseplants to your collection, look to the practical, but also into your heart.

Victorian Houseplant Resources

Consult these sites for more information about the plants discussed in this article, plus additional plants for those feeling bricky—that's nineteenth-century speak for bold!

Balcony Garden Web. "15 Victorian Era Houseplants That Britishers Grew." Accessed May 15, 2021. https://balconygardenweb.com /victorian-era-houseplants-indoors/.

Coulter, Lynn. "Historic Houseplants for Trendy Indoor Gardens." HGTV. April 20, 2018. https://www.hgtv.com/outdoors/flowers -and-plants/houseplants/historic-houseplants-for-trendy-indoor -gardens-pictures.

House Plant Hobbyist. "Plants of the Past: Popular Victorian House Plants." March 26, 2019. https://www.house-plant-hobbyist.com /blog/2019/3/15/plants-of-the-past-popular-victorian-house -plants.

Victorian Houseplant Care

Buckner, Heather. "Growing Citrus Indoors: Create a Little Slice of Paradise." Gardener's Path. December 23, 2019. https:// gardenerspath.com/plants/fruit-trees/grow-citrus-indoors/.

Grant, Bonnie L. "Victorian Indoor Plants: Caring For Old-Fashioned Parlor Plants." Gardening Know How. Last modified September 25, 2021. https://www.gardeningknowhow.com/houseplants /hpgen/victorian-indoor-plants.htm.

Group, Edward. "Absolute Beginner's Guide to Growing Your Own Aloe Vera." Global Healing. December 9, 2015. https://explore .globalhealing.com/guide-to-growing-your-own-aloe-vera/.

The Problem of Invasive Species

ᷡ Lupa ᷡ

Growing up as a child in the Midwestern United States, I spent a lot of time outside. I lived in a small town in a neighborhood that had been converted from farmland to housing several years before. Even the small patch of woods nearby was barely a remnant of what had once been there before European-American colonizers had arrived. But I drank it all in anyway, a lone lover of nature seeking wildness where I could.

I learned the names of as many of the plants as I could—chicory (*Cichorium intybus*) and Queen Anne's lace (*Daucus carota*), white clover (*Trifolium repens*) and red clover (*Trifolium pratense*), and white and yellow sweet

clover (*Melilotus albans* and *Melilotus officinalis*, respectively). Most were small herbs and forbs, but there was the occasional tree, like a sprawling tree of heaven (*Ailanthus altissima*) behind the back fence.

What I hadn't realized at the time was that none of these species were native. In fact, most of the plants I encountered were introduced from Europe or Asia. As I grew older and learned more about ecology, I discovered just how disruptive these plants really were to North American ecosystems. While they may have had many uses for human beings, they were wreaking havoc on other species.

A Few Terms

There are several terms that are used with regard to introduced species, whether plant, animal, or fungus:

Native Species: Native species have evolved for thousands of years in a particular ecosystem or region. They have deep, complex interrelationships with many other native species in their habitat, many of which we may not fully understand yet.

Non-Native Species: This simply means that a species did not evolve within this particular ecosystem. However, these species are not necessarily directly harmful to native species, and the term includes those that are cultivated in gardens, yards, and farms.

Naturalized Species: These are non-native species that have integrated into an ecosystem and are widespread enough that they are not likely to be eliminated. Many, though not all, naturalized species are invasive.

Invasive Species: Invasive species are those that are in direct competition with native species for food, space, and other resources, and they may lead to local or even total extinction of native species.

While non-native species that are not aggressively invasive may seem benign, keep in mind that every acre of land that has been turned into conventional farmland, housing developments, industrial areas, highways, and other human-dominated landscapes is one less acre of land available for native species. Moreover, because many invasive plants are very good at colonizing disturbed land (such as forests that have been clear-cut or land bulldozed for a housing subdivision), they can further prevent native plants from regaining ground. And when you consider that *habitat loss is the single biggest cause of species endangerment and extinction*, you begin to see how competition from invasive species adds to the pressure on threatened native ones.

Also please note that these terms are location-specific. Chicory is invasive in North America but native to much of Europe, western Asia, and northern Africa. The common dandelion (*Taraxacum officinale*) has some subspecies that are native to North America but others that have been introduced from Europe. And while Atlantic beach grass (*Ammophila breviligulata*) is native on the eastern seaboard, it has been introduced on much of the West Coast, where it aggressively displaces all the native dune plants for miles upon miles of beach.

How Do Invasive Species Harm Ecosystems?

There are a number of ways in which invasive species can wreak havoc on an ecosystem:

Replacing Important Food Sources

Plants have unique chemical compounds in them, and these compounds vary widely from species to species. The herbivores that eat them have evolved to digest these compounds. This includes not just larger vertebrate herbivores like deer and rabbits but also many herbivorous insects and other invertebrates. These invertebrates are an irreplaceable source of food for countless other species all through the food web; for example, 75 percent of what many baby birds eat in their first few weeks of life is insects and other arthropods.

Herbivores cannot just magically change their digestive systems to be able to eat non-native plants. Many invertebrates in particular are reliant on just a few native plant species. The caterpillar of the critically endangered Oregon silverspot butterfly (*Speyeria zerene hippolyta*), for example, can only eat the leaves of the early blue violet (*Viola adunca*). Just like we would get sick trying to eat the leaves of poisonous nightshade plants, these caterpillars would become ill and die from trying to feed on the invasive plants that have taken the place of the violets.

Crowding Out Native Species

Because many invasive plants and other species do not have natural predators here, they can take over large areas of land. This severely reduces habitat and other resources for native species, which still have to deal with the predators they evolved alongside. The competition from invasive species can even make the native ones go extinct, at least locally.

The aforementioned Atlantic beach grass and European beach grass (*Ammophila arenaria*) are good examples. American dune grass (*Leymus mollis*) is native to the Pacific Northwest's beaches. It normally grows in small patches with plenty of sand in between, which allows other native plants such as American sea rocket (*Cakile edentula*) and yellow sand verbena (*Abronia latifolia*) to grow and gives nesting space to birds like the threatened western snowy plover (*Charadrius nivosus nivosus*). However, the two invasive beach grass species form thick, unbroken fields that can stretch for many miles and leave no room for other plants nor sand for dune-nesting animals.

Directly Killing Native Species

Some invasive plants are so aggressive in their growth that they smother and kill other species. Kudzu (*Pueraria* spp.), Himalayan blackberry (*Rubus armeniacus*), and English ivy (*Hedera helix*) are all fast-growing plants that can take over many acres of land in just a few years. They crowd out and shade other plants, starving them of sunlight. And kudzu and ivy in particular can climb trees and shrubs, not only blocking their leaves from light, but even pulling smaller trees over from their sheer weight.

At least one invasive plant, the common reed (*Phragmites australis*) engages in chemical warfare. It releases an acidic compound from its roots that kills off any nearby plants. This allows it to take over more space without competition. Garlic mustard (*Alliaria petiolata*) is also thought to use the same tactic to conquer more territory.

The more native species that are removed from an ecosystem, the more vulnerable that ecosystem becomes. Each species is needed for the many relationships it has with others, whether as food, shelter, or even mutual support. When a species is crowded out by an invasive species, all of the strands it held in that complex web are destroyed, and the invader does little to nothing to pick up the pieces. If enough native species disappear, the ecosystem may collapse entirely, leading to the localized or entire extinction of even more native species, and leaving a desolate landscape with very little biodiversity save for a few of the most aggressive invasive species.

Sympathy for the Devil?

Invariably when the topic of invasive species comes up, there are always a few people who play devil's advocate. They may argue, for example, that the invasive plants are already here, and they didn't choose to be planted here, and that it's wrong to kill them off. Unfortunately, they have less empathy for the native species that are being displaced and killed by these invaders, whether directly or by the loss of important ecological partners. They can't look ahead to a potential future where entire ecosystems can be restored and saved by eradicating the non-native species and allowing the native ones to return and rebuild their ancient communities.

I've also heard the argument that since the invasive species have already made their home here, they should just be left alone to make their own place. Since they don't have any native predators to keep their numbers in check, though, it isn't likely that they're going to create a well-balanced community. And given that it took their predators back in their native home thousands of years to evolve the ability to eat them, it isn't likely that any new predators are going to evolve quickly enough here to keep them from destroying more native ecosystems. Occasionally, I'll run across someone who deliberately promotes and even spreads an invasive species because they "think it's pretty" (like a former neighbor of mine who let the Scotch broom on their land flourish even though it easily spread across property boundaries and was a continual nuisance for all the neighbors). Aesthetics are not more important than ecology, though, and a pretty garden is no replacement for a healthy, fully functioning native ecosystem that supports a wide range of biodiversity.

Finally, there's always That One Person who has to mention, "Well, humans are *the* most invasive species!" Ignoring, for the moment, the very real fact that much of the environmental destruction that has occurred over the past few hundred years is rooted in European colonialism and capitalism, rather than humanity as a whole, this argument is probably the worst one of the lot.* See, this situation is not either/or but both/and. Most environmentalists these days can accept these points:

1. Humans are the reason that invasive species are where they are in the first place, and certain groups of humans have historically been particularly adept at environmental destruction.

2. We here in the twenty-first century can take responsibility for the havoc that has been caused, and one way we can do that is do our best to try to restore damaged ecosystems to help make them more resilient for the future.

---

* This also gets into some very sticky territory surrounding the oppression of indigenous land management and ecological relationships by said colonial and capitalist forces, racist diversions along the lines of "Well, the earliest Native Americans probably caused the ice age megafauna here to go extinct, so they're just as bad as everyone else," and so on. All of this could very easily be several more articles, which we do not currently have the space for here.

In short, when you approach the problem of invasive species from an ecological perspective rather than a sentimental or misanthropic one, you understand the structure of how an ecosystem actually works and how an invasive species can absolutely break that structure. At that point, eradication of the invasive species becomes the most effective way to give that ecosystem a chance to recover.

Invasive Species in the United States

Some invasive species are particularly pernicious and have done a lot of damage to ecosystems here. Some were brought by early European colonizers as food or medicinal plants. Others were imported later as exotic additions to gardens, or for "beautifying" campaigns. Still others made their way here by accident, often in shipments of other plants. Many have made their way onto invasive species eradication lists in some states, and a few have even been banned from commercial sale. Here is a partial list of some of the most notorious:

Amur honeysuckle (*Lonicera maackii*)
Autumn olive (*Elaeagnus umbellata*)
'Bradford' pear (*Pyrus calleryana*)
Brazilian elodea (*Egeria densa*)
Bull thistle (*Cirsium vulgare*)
Butterfly bush (*Buddleja davidii*)
Cheatgrass (*Bromus tectorum*)
Cutleaf blackberry (*Rubus laciniatus*)
English ivy (*Hedera helix*)
Eurasian water milfoil (*Myriophyllum spicatum*)
European beach grass (*Ammophila arenaria*)
Garlic mustard (*Alliaria petiolata*)

Giant hogweed (*Heracleum mantegazzianum*)
Gorse (*Ulex europaeus*)
Himalayan blackberry (*Rubus armeniacus*)
Japanese barberry (*Berberis thunbergii*)
Japanese honeysuckle (*Lonicera japonica*)
Japanese knotweed (*Reynoutria japonica*)
Kudzu (*Pueraria* spp., especially *P. montana* var. *lobata*)
Morning glory/field bindweed (Convolvulaceae spp.,
    especially *Convolvulus arvensis*)
Norway maple (*Acer platanoides*)
Parrot feather (*Myriophyllum aquaticum*)
Purple loosestrife (*Lythrum salicaria*)
Reed canary grass (*Phalaris arundinacea*)
Russian thistle (*Kali tragus*)
Scotch broom (*Cytisus scoparius*)
Spotted jewelweed (*Impatiens capensis*)
Tree of heaven (*Ailanthus altissima*)
Water hyacinth (*Eichhornia crassipes*)
White waterlily/lily pad (*Nymphaea alba*)

While some of these and other plants that I have mentioned in this article may be edible or have medicinal or other uses, I strongly discourage deliberately planting them, especially in outdoor places where they may spread into wild ecosystems.

Choosing Native Species

This article has necessarily focused on the United States, partly because it is where I am most familiar ecologically and also due to a brevity of space. However, the following advice may be used by anyone wanting to propagate native species in their yard, garden, or other land.

How Do You Learn about Native Plants in Your Region?

Some entities to ask include plant nurseries; botany clubs (especially those specializing in native plants like the Native Plant Societies in many US states); botany, ecology, and related departments at colleges and universities; state and federal parks, wildlife refuges, forestry and natural resource departments, and other such governmental agencies; environmental organizations, especially those with a local or regional focus; and online groups on Facebook and other platforms focusing on native plants, especially in your state, country, or other area. Many field guides to local and regional plants also focus predominantly on native species. If you use iNaturalist, a free nature identification app for all smartphones, you can search projects at inaturalist.org/projects to see if anyone has organized a project for identifying native plants where you are.

What Native Plants Currently Grow in Your Area?

Once you've familiarized yourself with some of your native flora, see if you can identify which ones are found locally. This may be tougher if you're in a more developed area, but give it a try anyway. iNaturalist and field guides can be good aids for identification.

What Plants Historically Grew in Your Area?

If your neighborhood is primarily full of non-native plants, do some research to find out what was there before it was developed. You may want to ask local governmental, academic, or environmental entities for information about what ecosystems were historically found where you are.

What Animals, Especially Insects and Other Invertebrates, Are Found in Your Area?

They are the ones who need the support of native plants the most, and while you may not be able to give them complete ecosystems, just offering a little habitat or food may be enough of an oasis to help a native species hang on. Perhaps in the future a larger habitat restoration will happen, and your little island's inhabitants can help repopulate it.

How Much Room Do You have?

Be realistic about the space you have. You may not be able to plant several large trees, for example, but if you can add a variety of smaller flowering native plants to your garden or yard, that can become a mini ecosystem on its own. Pay attention to which plants thrive best in your soil, lighting, and microclimate and which ones may need a little help with soil augmentation or extra watering.

———

Finally, once you've planted your native garden, don't be alarmed if you find that insects and other animals have been chewing on them. That's a good sign! It means that native animals have likely discovered their favorite foods, and you're giving them a chance to survive in an increasingly dangerous world.

This is just a very brief introduction to native plants; if you'd like to discuss the subject further, please feel free to contact me at lupa.greenwolf@gmail.com.

Wild Tobacco and Other Insecticidal Plants

❧ Diana Rajchel ❧

In Michigan, the first property I lived on had a creek running through the backyard that displayed such natural wonders as swimming ducks, evil geese, and the occasional chaotic muskrat. While that appeared idyllic as the late spring snows of 2020 melted away, the sudden surge of sun-awakened mosquitoes brought Vivaldi's "The Four Seasons" playing in my head to a screeching halt. The buggers invaded the house before the snow melted!

While my partner and I acknowledged the temptation to bomb our little plot of land in DEET, our aggravation with the biting insects did not make us forget the potential health consequences of doing so, especially

to our kids. In part because I finally had room to do so, but also to make sure our family had food during the uncertain times of that spring, I had started a bucket garden, and it was important that the harvest stay edible, thus the need to fight nature with nature.

The list in this article is far from exhaustive—botanists and other biological researchers are constantly discovering new traits of old plants and new plants with new traits altogether. I chose these herbs because the seeds and rhizomes are accessible, most are easy to grow, and farmers and gardeners have used them long enough to share consistent information about their application as insecticides. Much of what we know comes from researchers testing the essential oils. The average home-grower doesn't have the time or the equipment to distill pure extracts, but home herbalists can make their own repellents from most of these plants via tinctures and maceration. You can also plant them near other plants that may not share the natural defenses of their siblings.

Wild Tobacco

My partner, an avid naturalist, had a suggestion for the bucket garden: wild tobacco. Wild tobacco is a bit hard to source—I finally found a medicinal herbs seed catalog, after much digging—and is also difficult to start because it requires scarification (a scratching of the seed wall) to germinate. Given how tiny tobacco seeds are, this is not an easy process.

The difficult and delicate seeding pays off once the plant takes root and flowers. Mosquitoes, drawn by the flowers, suckle on the nicotine, become addicted, and die. While wild tobacco self-pollinates, it also draws pollinators such as hummingbirds and bees. While other exposed creatures do appear to experience nicotine addiction, it doesn't kill them the way it does mosquitoes. (I am uncertain of the ethics of addicting pollinators to nicotine.) Despite giving bees nicotine fits, it appears that the chemical also helps them recognize nourishing flowers faster.

Wild tobacco is highly toxic, and once it gets going, it's best to leave it near a mosquito-heavy part of the yard, far away from pets, children, and curious passersby. Unfortunately, for some gardeners, the toxicity and ethics may be too much to balance. Fortunately, there are plenty of less dangerous and easier-to-grow plants that can also kill invasive insects.

Garlic

Researchers have found that garlic distilled into an essential oil acts as an effective poison against mealworms. Even better, it has almost no toxicity to humans or pets. Given its global ubiquity as a flavoring agent and medicine, getting your bulbs for growth takes little more than a trip to the grocery store. Plenty of absent-minded people have bought that bulb of garlic and then, distracted from what we meant to cook, wound up with a green sprout emerging from it!

Some experimental gardeners have planted garlic between rows of more vulnerable plants to good effect. If you enjoy companion planting, explore what makes good neighbors for garlic—it's often the very plants that you want to have for dinner before the mites do!

Wormwood

Most members of the *Artemisia* genus have insect-repelling and insect-killing properties. The most famous of these, wormwood (yes, the sort added to absinthe's distillation, *A. absinthium*), can repel fleas, slugs, and flies. If mixed in an alcohol solution, it can simply end them. Researchers found that an alcohol-based spray made from wormwood essential oil can kill garden mites and other pests that eat away at common plants, according to the *Journal of Insect Science*.

Green Chilies

Green chilies, and really all chilies, make wonderful insecticides—they evolved for it! The hot taste you get from chilies and peppers developed as a way of signaling "don't eat me!" to bugs. Plant them in the same rows as the plants that insects and critters tend to raid. Most find the bite-back a deterrent. If they remain determined, an extract made from tincturing the chilies in vinegar or alcohol sprayed lightly on the plants that need protection drives them off fast. Pests that try again after that chomp tend to only survive a few days after trying a bite of chili.

Peppermint and Spearmint

Mint does wonderful things: clears the sinuses, freshens breath, and flavors delicious food, to name just a few of its talents. But, for years, I wondered why I never needed to shake insects out of any of my mints. Digging into agricultural research on biodegradable insecticides explained why: the active chemical in mints, menthol, is deadly to weevils and grain-borer insects. If you are trying to grow wheat, corn, oats, and so on, having a few pots of mint at the base of the plants may drive off some of the more persistent invaders.

Do not plant mints in the ground unless that's the only thing you want growing there. The rootstock spreads fast and is highly invasive—keep mint in pots!

Ginger

Garlic and ginger always seem to pair together in my refrigerator, often because between the two of them, they cover just about any run-of-the-mill cough, cold, or antibacterial need. Moreover, as researchers struggling to fight off brown planthoppers in rice paddies found in the *Annals of Parasitology*, it also teams up with chilies to kill off bugs—with far less environmental fallout than what comes with mineral-based commercial pesticides. Most people can buy ginger from the produce section at their grocery store. Cut any root you get from the store into one-inch pieces, and then let it soak in room-temperature water overnight to remove any chemicals meant to prevent growth. Take the ginger out of the water and dry it for two days so that the cuts can heal. Then, plant in loose soil near the plants you want it to protect.

Tapping into Insecticidal Plants

Determined gardeners have a few approaches they can take when driving off the flying hordes. My preferred method is proximity: I raise the plant with the insecticide goodness and place it near the plants needing extra protection. Between-row planting maximizes space use and reduces problems with pests. You can also process the not-toxic-to-humans plants at home and create sprays or insecticidal soaps.

If you decide to make your own insecticide, consider the type of bugs that munch on your garden and what works best against them. While it's tempting to create a catch-all spray, you may end up harming your plants if you don't pay attention to their needs *and* the troubles that tend to beset them.

⚘ Insecticide Soap

A good base formula for insecticide soap is as follows:

> 1 cup apple cider vinegar
>
> 1 cup liquid soap, without a degreaser added (degreasers can dry out your plants)
>
> ½ cup vodka or other alcohol
>
> 1 tablespoon essential oil or herbal extract of your choice

Mix all ingredients in a standard spray bottle that you can buy at any garden supply.

When using homegrown insecticides, keep in mind that most work slower than commercial chemical mixes. While insect death is often instantaneous from traditional methods, it comes more slowly when using essential oils and plant extracts. So have some patience. The chemical mix from your own hand is, in theory, less harsh, and that means that the insects may get a few extra bites in on their way out. The payoff for the delayed gratification of a less bug-bitten garden haul is healthier, safer vegetables and fruits to eat, and knowing that the approach you took is a lot more sustainable than agricultural methods that emerged from the Industrial Revolution.

The plants that you can distill into insecticides also work as repellents, especially if you grew the plants as part of your guardians of the garden.

Resources

American Chemical Society. "Tobacco and Its Evil Cousin Nicotine Are Good as a Pesticide." ACS News Service Weekly PressPac, October 27, 2010. https://www.acs.org/content/acs/en/pressroom/presspacs/2010/acs-presspac-october-27-2010/tobacco-and-its-evil-cousin-nicotine-are-good-as-a-pesticide.html.

Cheraghi Niroumand, Mina, Mohammad Hosein Farzaei, Elahe Karimpour Razkenari, Gholamreza Amin, Mahnaz Khanavi, Tahmineh Akbarzadeh, and Mohammad Reza Shams-Ardekani. "An Evidence-Based Review on Medicinal Plants Used as Insecticide and Insect Repellent in Traditional Iranian Medicine." *Iranian Red Crescent Medical Journal* 18, no. 2 (2016): e22361. doi:10.5812/ircmj.22361.

Cook, Robert. "Plant-Based Insect Repellent." Permaculture Research Institute. January 7, 2016. https://www.permaculturenews.org/2016/01/07/plant-based-insect-repellents/.

Kalia. "Plant Extracts as Natural Insecticides." American Museum of Natural History. Accessed September 4, 2021. https://www.amnh.org/learn-teach/curriculum-collections/young-naturalist-awards/winning-essays/2011/plant-extracts-as-natural-insecticides.

Madreseh-Ghahfarokhi, S., Y. Pirali, A. Dehghani-Samani, and A. Dehghani-Samani. "The Insecticidal and Repellent Activity of Ginger (*Zingiber officinale*) and Eucalyptus (*Eucalyptus globulus*) Essential Oils against *Culex theileri* Theobald, 1903 (Diptera: Culicidae)." *Annals of Parasitology* 64, no. 4 (2018): 351–60. doi:10.17420/ap6404.171.

Queen Mary University of London. "Nicotine Enhances Bees' Activity." ScienceDaily. May 16, 2017. https://www.sciencedaily.com/releases/2017/05/170516080757.htm.

Zhang, Ning, Liang Tang, Wei Hu, Kun Wang, You Zhou, Hong Li, Congling Huang, Jiong Chun, and Zhixiang Zhang. "Insecticidal, Fumigant, and Repellent Activities of Sweet Wormwood Oil and Its Individual Components against Red Imported Fire Ant Workers (Hymenoptera: Formicidae)." *Journal of Insect Science* 14 (2014): 241. doi:10.1093/jisesa/ieu103.

Cooking

At a Sultan's Table

≫ James Kambos ≪

From the fourteenth to the early twentieth centuries, the Ottoman Empire controlled a vast region of the world. It stretched from Austria to the Persian Gulf and from the Arabian Peninsula west to Algeria in North Africa.

The head of the empire was the sultan. The sultans ruled with absolute authority from their imperial home, Topkapi Palace, located in modern-day Istanbul, Turkey. Topkapi Palace and Istanbul weren't just the center of the Ottoman government; they were also the center of some of the most sophisticated cooking the world has ever known.

One of the keys to the success of the Ottoman Empire was its ability to control some of the world's most vital trade routes. These trade routes connected the lands of the east with Europe. Great wealth traveled along these routes—luxurious fabrics, precious metals, and gems—plus herbs, spices, and other flavorings. Some of these herbs and spices found their way to the many kitchens of Topkapi Palace, where chefs skillfully blended them into dishes that were served on many a sultan's table over the centuries. Some were also used by palace physicians to help ease many medical conditions.

As the empire expanded, the Ottomans left their culinary imprint on many regions. But the Ottomans also had a high regard for the food and recipes of the nations they conquered. As a result, they would frequently incorporate these new ideas into their native cuisine. What began as the regional cuisine of the Anatolian region spread. With the help of local influences, many of these foods and herbs are still enjoyed today. This is why you can enjoy some similar foods and seasonings at a café in Istanbul, Athens, or Beirut. But you'll find differences depending on the locale. For example, a Greek cook preparing stuffed grape leaves may include currants. A Lebanese cook may omit the currants but include chopped tomato instead. Both are delicious and different but from the same culinary family.

There is some debate about which recipes and herbs the Ottomans actually created or discovered. Some argue that the Ottomans only borrowed many of these foods from other cultures. We may never know for sure. We do know that the sultan's royal court employed a number of chefs, likely from different regions, who perfected many of these recipes, adding their own culinary knowledge. Considering the size of the far-reaching Ottoman Empire, we also know that the sultans, and their military campaigns, helped spread and influence the herbs used, the cooking styles, and the cuisine of many nations.

Among those who were influenced by the Ottomans' culinary style was my grandmother, Katina. During her youth, the Greek island she was raised on in the Aegean Sea just off the Turkish coast was part of the Ottoman Empire. Long after she immigrated to the United States, my grandmother, whom we called *Yiayia*, never failed to cook in her Greek-Ottoman style. Although I didn't realize it as a child, most of the food I enjoyed was the same food served on the sultans' table.

Ottoman Flavors

Here are some herbs and flavorings enjoyed by the sultan's imperial court and how they were and are still used. I've also found it necessary to mention rice. According to most herbal authorities, since rice is a grass it's also considered an herb. Rice, as you'll see, remains an important ingredient in Ottoman/Turkish cuisine.

Keep in mind these herbs, spices, and flavorings were first served at the sultan's table. They were also enjoyed by the visiting dignitaries, and very likely the women of the harem. Eventually, these seasonings found their way to the tables of the working classes. Then, due to trade and military conquest, these herbs and spices became integrated into the cuisines of the various Ottoman nations. Even today this culinary bond remains strong among countries that were once part of the Ottoman Empire.

The chefs in the sultan's court were probably familiar with about forty or more herbs and spices. I'm going to share what I consider the top ten most used. They're also the ones I remember being used in my grandmother's kitchen when I was a child.

Basil

This Iranian native adapted well to Turkey's climate. It is used frequently in Turkish food. Prized for its sweet and savory blend of flavors, it goes well in meat and tomato dishes. Add it to a recipe as the Turks do, near the end of the cooking time. That way it keeps its fresh green color and delicate flavor.

Bay

Bay is the leaf of the bay laurel tree. Turkish bay leaves are among the finest in the world, which explains why Turkey exports thousands of tons each year. Use it to add depth of flavor to stews and soups. Bay leaves are brittle and tough. For this reason, always remove and discard bay leaves when the dish is finished cooking.

Cinnamon

The Ottomans used cinnamon in both desserts and main courses. It's still frequently used in meat and vegetable dishes, where it adds a warm note.

Dill

This fragrant herb with a delicate, feathery foliage and a bright, fresh taste was and still is found in Turkish vegetable and cheese dishes. It is frequently blended with olive oil and used to dress a variety of vegetables.

Lemon

Lemons have been used since Ottoman times to flavor soups and fillings for stuffed vegetables, and wedges of fresh lemon were used to accompany fish dishes.

Mastic

Also known as gum mastic, mastic is a resin obtained from the small mastic tree grown on the Greek Aegean island of Chios, my grandmother's home. In August and September the mastic resin is harvested by cutting gashes in the tree's trunk. Pieces of resin, or "tears," fall to the ground and harden. The tears are cleaned by hand, which takes a long time and makes mastic expensive: a pound costs over a hundred dollars.

The Ottomans loved mastic. Most mastic was sent to Topkapi Palace, where it was chewed in its natural state or used in candy (Turkish delight, or *lokum*), alcoholic beverages, and medicines. The women of the sultan's harem used to chew it before spending the night with the sultan—it had a reputation as an aphrodisiac.

Mastic is still enjoyed today around the Near East. It has a unique taste that's hard to describe. Some say it tastes like a pine forest, and that's pretty close. My yiayia always had a jar of the resin pieces in her kitchen. I was encouraged to chew it because yiayia said it was good for my teeth. Now, decades later, according to dental research, it turns out she was right: it can help reduce bacteria in the mouth that contribute to cavities.

Mint

Refreshing mint was highly regarded by the Ottomans and is still used today. It makes a superb tea. It's also used to add a bright, fresh taste to salads and fillings for vegetables and grape leaves.

Parsley

The broadleaf variety is very popular and has been used since the Ottoman era. It can be found in soup, stews, salads, and fillings for vegetables.

Rice

Rice is probably the most popular grain and herb used by the Ottomans. The sultan's cooks were known to use over 200 tons of rice in a year. Flavored with other herbs, used in stuffings, or prepared with meat, rice is still popular in the eastern Mediterranean today.

Rose and Rose Water

Delicate and fragrant, rose petals and rose water were favorite flavorings used during the Ottoman rule. Rose petals were made into an exquisite sweet preserve you can still buy today. Rose water was blended into syrups, which were used in beverages or to pour over pastries. Rose is still used as a flavor for lokum candy.

Dolma: Food Fit for a Sultan

Dolma refers to any vegetable or leaf that is stuffed with or wrapped around a filling. The vegetables are hollowed out first, then filled. The leaves, such as grape leaves or cabbage leaves, are wrapped around a small portion of the filling. Vegetables used include eggplant, peppers, zucchini, and tomatoes. The filling could be rice, rice and meat, onions, or cheese. The filling is always seasoned with herbs. Some experts say dolma originated in Greece or present-day Iran. Some say Turkey. However, we do know the Ottomans became quite fond of them and raised them to a culinary artform that they helped spread around their empire.

Originally, dolma were reserved as a food for the sultan and his guests only. Eventually, the working classes enjoyed them too. Dolma can be served as a main dish, a side dish, or an appetizer known as *meze*.

My personal favorite is stuffed grape leaves. I remember when I was a boy, in late spring or early summer my aunt Ethel would take my grandmother and me out to the back hill country near our home in Southern Ohio to handpick the grape leaves.

We'd jump into my aunt's old black and white Rambler and drive along country lanes until we'd find the wild grape vines climbing up trees or over weathered fences. My grandmother would lead us as she picked the perfect leaves, which were destined to hold her heavenly filling. We usually remained silent as we performed this annual ritual surrounded by the sweet, honeysuckle-scented air on warm spring or summer Ohio afternoons all those years ago.

Then we'd drive back to my aunt's house. In the kitchen my grandmother would first blanch the leaves to soften them. Then she'd go out to the garden and cut fresh dill and mint. Soon the kitchen was perfumed with the scents of dill, mint, and sautéed onion. Then these ingredients would be blended with parboiled rice. Working quickly, my grandmother's experienced hands would wrap each leaf around a bit of the filling. After simmering a short time, the dolma would arrive at the table, where they'd be served with a squeeze of lemon or a dollop of homemade yogurt. As we ate them, I didn't realize it then, but the food I was eating was at one time food served only to the sultan.

Decades later, the scent of stuffed grape leaves simmering is with me still. That scent reminds me of the essence of summer afternoons so long ago.

The following stuffed grape leaves recipe is one I've perfected and is close to my grandmother's. Today I use grape leaves that are packed in a jar. It's less time consuming and safer.

⚘ Stuffed Grape Leaves

These dolma are scented with lemon, dill, mint, and parsley. You may serve them as an appetizer along with cheeses, olives, and other types of dolma. Some people can make this an entire meal, or they serve them as a side dish. You may eat them warm or at room temperature.

Serve with a squeeze of lemon or a bit of plain yogurt spooned over them. They're also good plain. And, yes, you do eat the leaves, not just the filling.

You will need:

1 jar of grape leaves (you will need about 3 dozen leaves, or a few more)

1 large onion, finely chopped

4 tablespoons olive oil, plus 4 tablespoons

1 cup rice

¼ cup finely chopped fresh parsley

2 tablespoons chopped fresh dill, or 1½ teaspoons dried dill

1 tablespoon chopped fresh mint, or ¾ teaspoon dried mint

½ teaspoon salt

Optional delicious additions to the filling (choose 1):

¼ cup currants

¼ cup pine nuts

1 small tomato, peeled, seeded, and chopped

1 cup water, plus 1 cup

6 tablespoons lemon juice

1½ cups stock: beef, chicken, or vegetable

Lemon wedges for garnish, or to squeeze on the dolma if you wish

Before cooking the dolma, the grape leaves must be blanched to remove excess brine and to soften them. To do this, bring a pot of water to a boil, then turn the heat off. Add about half the leaves at a time. Let them soak for 10–15 minutes. Using a slotted spoon, remove the leaves and place them in a large bowl of cool water. When leaves are cool enough to handle, place them on paper towels. Pat dry and lay them on a plate. If you notice any leaves that have a large tough stem, cut it off. Last, set aside 3 or 4 large leaves; I'll explain later how these will be used.

For the filling, sauté the onion in 4 tablespoons of the oil in a large frying pan until soft. Now add rice, herbs, salt, any optional ingredient, and 1 cup of water. Bring to a boil. Cover and simmer for 10 minutes. The rice will *not* be done yet. Let cool.

Next, place the 3 or 4 leaves you set aside earlier in the bottom of a 3-quart saucepan. This will prevent scorching. Now we begin to stuff the leaves.

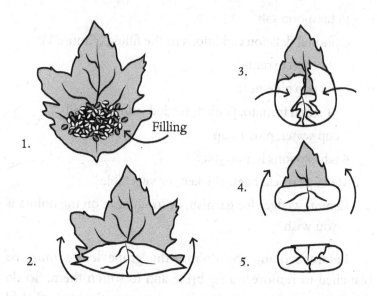

1.
Filling
2.
3.
4.
5.

Take a leaf, one at a time, and place it on a plate. The dull, veined side should face up. Place 1 rounded teaspoon of the filling mixture in the middle of each leaf. Roll the bottom of the leaf first, up and over the filling. Fold the sides of the leaf in, over the filling. Continue rolling up. Don't roll them too tightly, as the rice needs some room to expand while the rolls simmer.

Arrange the dolma seam-side down in the saucepan you prepared earlier. You'll have 2 or 3 layers when finished. Sprinkle with lemon juice and the remaining olive oil. Pour the stock *and* the remaining 1 cup of water over the dolma. So the rolls don't come loose during cooking, place a small heat-proof dish or saucer on top of the rolls. Cover and simmer for about 35 minutes. Cool in the pan. Serve in any of the ways I mentioned earlier. Makes about 3 dozen dolma.

Rice: Turkish Pilav

I feel I should provide a recipe for the Turkish pilav (pilaf), because rice pilaf was served as a side dish at almost every meal eaten by the sultans. Under orders from the sultans, rice was grown in Turkey. Unlike most rice served in the West, the rice in Turkish pilaf is lightly sautéed first. This will give it an extra depth of flavor. Serve it as a side dish with meats, kebabs, or with stew spooned over it.

You will need:

2 tablespoons butter, plus 4 tablespoons butter melted, set aside

1 cup white rice, long or medium grain

2 cups (1 can) chicken broth

½ teaspoon salt (optional)

Freshly ground black pepper to taste

In a 2- or 3-quart saucepan, melt the 2 tablespoons of butter over medium heat. Don't let it brown. Add the rice and stir for 2 or 3 minutes, until each grain glistens and looks translucent. The rice should not look brown. Pour in the broth and add the salt and pepper. Bring to a full boil, stirring the rice once or twice. Cover the pan, reduce heat to its lowest temperature, and simmer for about 20 minutes. Never stir the rice as it simmers. The rice is done when small holes appear on top of the rice and the liquid is absorbed. It should be tender but slightly firm to the bite.

Remove the rice from the heat and pour the reserved 4 tablespoons of melted butter over the rice. Toss gently with a fork until the rice glistens. Now, for fluffy rice, remove the lid and drape a cotton kitchen towel over the pan. Let sit at room temperature for about 15 minutes. Serve. Makes 4 to 6 servings.

Sweet Endings

Every meal served at a sultan's table ended in elegant style. Rather than serving heavy cakes, the Ottoman sultans preferred to end their meals with small elegant sweets. For dessert, the table would be set with silver candy dishes filled with the Ottoman specialty lokum. These small sweets would be generously dusted with powdered sugar. Most likely they were flavored with mastic or rose. Of course, trays of baklava filled with chopped pistachios would appear, and it would be bathed in syrups of honey, rose, or citrus.

After the meal, small cups of Turkish coffee would be served. It wouldn't be unusual if the coffee was served in dazzling small cups set with diamonds.

The power of the Ottoman Empire and the sultans who ruled it gradually faded, but the influence of those once-mighty sultans can still be felt and tasted today in a cuisine that they helped shape and create.

Stocks and Broths

⇜ Dawn Ritchie ⇝

Stock is a liquid base used for soups, stews, and sauces that is derived from the nutrients in food scraps (bones, vegetable peels and ends). These leftovers, which normally end up in the trash, are a treasure trove of nutrition and flavor for the knowing cook. No carcass should ever end up in the green bin without first being tossed in a stock pot. Along with a few aromatics, herbs, spices, and water, you can turn those useless remainders into future meals. Stock is a high-value resource that is frugal and flavorful and avoids waste.

Respect Your Ingredients

Making stock not only furthers your grocery budget, but it also respects the creatures and vegetation that provide for your family. That may sound clichéd, but when you approach your food with this consideration in mind, you'll honor those gifts of nature by deriving every ounce of benefit from them. What you get in return is a flavor bomb that ups your culinary cred to chef status.

You will find huge pots of stock simmering away in virtually every fine restaurant kitchen. Anytime a chef adds liquid to a dish, they look to their stock supply. And you can too. That means rice, pasta, grains, gravies, soups, stews, sauces, potatoes, and more. You can even steam your vegetables with it. Wonder why restaurant dining is so superior? Stock is the secret. Once you start using stock instead of plain water and discover how it rocks the flavor of your meals, you'll never look back.

The Base Components of Stock

Stock is a combination of aromatic vegetables (mirepoix), herbs (a bouquet garni), spice (peppercorns), and water. To that you add your main ingredient. For a beef, seafood, or poultry stock, you will add bones. For a vegetable stock, you simply add more vegetables.

Mirepoix

Mirepoix is the aromatic ingredient—a collection of chopped onions, celery, and carrots. You'll want one and a half onions to every carrot and celery rib. These are some of the least expensive vegetables you can buy yet the most consequential. They are used in many gourmet cooking recipes merely for aromatic enhancement, then discarded before serving.

Bouquet Garni

These are your standard herbs—thyme, parsley, and bay leaf. Tie sprigs of these herbs together in a bundle with kitchen string and you have the classic French *bouquet garni*. Making a bundle ensures that your herbs aren't floating around when you try to skim scum off the top of the stockpot. If you have a sunny windowsill, consider potting up these herbs so you can snip and go. They bring soothing greenery and aroma to your kitchen and meals. If not, there's always store-bought.

Spice

Whole black peppercorns are your primary spice. They offer a bit of complexity. But you can personalize your stock for your signature dishes with other whole spices like coriander or fennel seeds if you wish. We'll get to that later.

Bones

Precooked or freshly roasted bones are generally used for stock. Using the carcass of a roast chicken after a family meal is a good example. Pre-roasting raw beef marrow bones is another. Roasted bones deliver a deeper, more robust flavor. For fish, sweat the bones in a dry hot sauté pan before adding them to your stock pot.

Begin with the Best

Grass-fed beef, wild-caught white fish, free-range chicken, and organic veggies will ensure that you are concentrating whatever is inside those throwaway scraps down to their purest essence. A free-roaming chicken allowed to wander and scratch for bugs, worms, and vegetation will enjoy a diverse diet that develops the healthy building blocks of life from bones to breast.

A grass-fed cow will grow to maturity eating crude proteins, vitamins, and minerals from its natural forage instead of a bucket of acid-stomach feed that was formulated to quickly bulk up a bovine for sale, not nourish it.

The same holds for your vegetables. Ensure they are clean and healthy selections. I use non-GMO, organic vegetables and grow my own. If you plant a backyard or patio garden, making stock is a good reason to get carrots, onions, and celery into the ground. They are the starting lineup for all stocks.

Regrow organic celery you've purchased by cutting off the chunky bulb end, setting it in water until it sprouts roots, and replanting in moist soil. Water liberally and harvest individual ribs as they grow to feed your stock pot.

The Difference between Stocks and Broths

The prevailing wisdom is that broth is made from meat cast-offs while stock is prepared from bones. But it also has something to do with heat. Stocks should remain clear with a translucent, gelatinous viscosity when cooled, while broth is looser and cloudier in appearance. This is because the slow heat used in stock-making draws all the collagen, glutamine, gelatin, and other minerals out of the skeletal structure of foul, beef, and seafood—nutrients that are good for your body and gut. Broth comes to a full boil and is quicker to make but doesn't possess the same level of gelatinous consistency. Of course, seldom do you get a bone without just a little bit of meat on it, so maintaining that simmer is crucial. If your stock does come to a hard boil, as broths do, you will see your liquid turn cloudy. It will still be edible, just less desirable.

Demi-glace

You can reduce your stock by half by cooking it down to a *demi-glace*, which is more concentrated in color and flavor. Demi-glace will also take up less room to store. Freeze your demi-glace in smaller portions because you won't need a whole jar to add to a sauce. You could put it into a freezer bag and freeze it flat, chipping off only what you need, or pour it into ice cube trays to store the cubes—a technique I use for my homemade pesto every summer.

When I make a prime cut steak, I often heat up an ice cube of demi-glace, sometimes even reducing it further down to a "glace," then spoon it out onto a plate and lay the steak on top. I can't even describe how delicious this is. It is five-star restaurant quality.

Take It Slow

While stocks require a long-haul process to make, it really isn't a difficult one. You toss bones, your aromatics, herbs, and spices into a pot of cool water, turn up the heat, and let it simmer for hours. The magic is all happening in the background while you go about your day. Most likely you will forget about it until you enter the kitchen and smell the steamy goodness of the effort that comes with preparing for your future sustenance. I consider making stocks self-care. I'm not only frugal but also thoughtful about what goes into my body and how my food tastes. Once you realize how easy stock is to make, you'll regret having ever spent two dollars on a small box of sodium and preservative-filled stock.

The Remains of the Day

If you aren't up to making a pot of stock when you've finished your roast beef or chicken, store the bones in a freezer bag in your freezer. Then, on a lazy Sunday, get a pot going. Plan on a minimum six-hour simmer. (If you use a pressure cooker, reduce that time by four and a half hours.)

Storing Stock

You can store stock in your refrigerator for a week or in the freezer for three months, or preserve it in canning jars to make it shelf-stable. Before canning, skim the fat off, decant the stock into hot sterilized jars, leaving one inch of headspace, screw on the two-piece lids, and process the jars in your canner for twenty minutes.

I use the freezer option because I use my stock regularly. In fact, one of my freezer shelves is devoted solely to pint-size mason jars of stocks. When it's full, I truly feel wealthy. It's the same experience as venturing into your pantry filled with preserves that you put up for the winter. That jar of mustard pickles. Pot of jam. Baggies of dehydrated mushrooms, fruit leather, or dilly beans. You feel taken care of. You feel abundant. You feel smart.

If you use glass mason jars and plan to freeze, as I do, choose wide-mouthed pint-size thick-walled jars. Leave an inch of expansion space at the top. I have never had a hardy pint-size jar break in the freezer. The thin-walled jars or quart-size are less reliable but fine for canner processing. You can also save your stock in plastic containers or use the ice cube method.

Okay, let's make some stock.

ᴥ Vegetable Stock Recipe

This is the easiest one to prepare because it doesn't use bones and cooks faster. It's also a great use for the trimmings from your vegetables. I keep leftover vegetable scraps (onion, carrot, celery cut-offs, parsnip peels, leek tops, fennel bulbs, mushroom stems, etc.) in my vegetable crisper. When I have enough, into the stock pot they go, and in the matter of an hour I have a new jar of liquid gold to add to my pantry. It costs nothing and the end result is far superior to store-bought.

You can also make stock on demand from fresh raw vegetables any time you wish. Just give them a rough chop to expose as much of the vegetable to the water as possible and you will draw out all that veggie goodness.

Gather ahead:

> Stock pot
>
> Knife and cutting board
>
> Water
>
> Vegetables
>
> Herbs and peppercorns
>
> Spoon
>
> Fine mesh sieve
>
> Storage container of your choice
>
> Canner (if you choose to can it and store it on a shelf)

For a standard vegetable stock, you will need:

> 2 large carrots
>
> 2 ribs celery
>
> 3 medium onions

2–3 sprigs thyme

3–4 sprigs parsley

1–2 bay leaves

6–8 whole black peppercorns

Cool water

There really is no predetermined number of veggies for a vegetable stock. You will generally want 1½ onions to every 1 rib of celery and 1 carrot. The volume of water is determined by the number of veggies. Add just enough cool water to cover them for a heartier stock, or add more water for a lighter, milder stock.

You can also design your own unique vegetable stock that suits your personal taste or culture by playing with the ingredients and spices. Experiment!

Potential Vegetable, Herb, and Spice Additions

Fennel bulb

Leeks

Mushrooms (adds umami)

Chard

Corn cobs

Parsnip

Garlic

Ginger (skin left on)

Asparagus ends

Kombu

Nori

Peppers

Tomatoes or a bit of paste

Parmesan rinds (also adds umami)

Cilantro

Tarragon

Dill

Chervil

Basil

Lemongrass

Sage

Saffron threads

Rosemary

White peppercorns

Coriander seeds

What to Avoid
Avoid starchy vegetables like potatoes or squash that will break down and turn your stock cloudy. Some vegetables can also turn your stock slightly bitter. Brassicas, artichokes, and green beans are a few to avoid.

Leave Out the Salt
Some cooks do add salt to their stock, but beware—as the stock reduces, it will concentrate that saltiness. The better choice is to season your dish after you use your stock. It will afford you more control over the outcome.

Pre-roasting Vegetables (Optional)
It's not a necessary step, but you can toss your vegetables with a small amount of cooking oil and sauté them in a pan or roast

them in the oven on a sheet pan at 325°F until caramelized for a more robust flavor prior to adding them to the stock pot.

The Basic Steps

Chop your veggies and add them to your stock pot. Cover with cool water. Turn the heat up to medium-high. Add in the herbs and spices of your choice. When the water begins to steam and bubbles break the surface, lower to a simmer. Cook for 1 hour minimum, longer for a reduction.

Skim off any scum that may appear on the surface. Strain out the solids using a fine sieve. Jar up. Cool before storing.

Bone Stocks

Introducing bones to the stockpot means you will be winging your recipe even more. It's not likely you can correctly measure a cup of bones, so look to ratios. Remember, the bones are the star of the show, and the mirepoix (onions, carrots, celery) are your supporting players. The ratio of bones to mirepoix is 3:1 minimum. That means 3 parts bones to 1 part mirepoix. More bones, more intense beef, fish, or poultry flavor.

ᾧ Beef Stock

Beef bones (knuckles, marrow, shanks, neck bones, oxtail, etc.)

Mirepoix (onions, celery, carrot)

Cooking oil

Bouquet garni (thyme, parsley, bay leaf bundle)

6–8 peppercorns

Water to cover

Begin by tossing your bones and mirepoix lightly with cooking oil and roasting them in the oven on a sheet pan at a high heat (425°F) for around 45 minutes. Check them occasionally and give them a turn or two. Once the bones are browned and the vegetables are caramelized, add them to your stock pot along with the bouquet garni and peppercorns and cover with cool water (never hot).

Deglaze the sheet pan with water or red wine and add that to the stock pot. There's added value there.

Turn up the heat, bring it barely to a boil, then immediately reduce heat to simmer for 6–8 hours, ensuring the liquid never returns to a rolling boil. Tiny bubbles should just barely break the surface at the edges.

Strain, jar up, and store.

Chicken Stock

Chicken bones and frame

Mirepoix (onions, celery, carrot)

Bouquet garni (thyme, parsley, bay leaf bundle)

6–8 peppercorns

Water to cover

The same ratio of bones to mirepoix (3:1) applies to chicken stock. You can pre-roast your bones (as in the beef recipe) or just add all ingredients directly to your pot and simmer for 8 hours. Strain, jar, and store.

Fish Stock

This stock is the base for dishes like bouillabaisse, chowders, risottos, steamed mussels, lobster bisque, calamari, paella, fish soup and stew, clam dishes, poaching sauce, and other flavored sauces for seafood entrées.

This is also the stock where you get to employ those lesser-used herbs that often collect dust on your spice shelf—tarragon, dill, fennel seeds, and white peppercorns, for example. Fish stock is a great way to utilize the bones and fish heads of seafood, especially if you have an angler in the family or if you tend to buy your fish whole and fillet it yourself. It eliminates waste and adds *fumet* (aroma), as the French say, to your cooking arsenal.

Use white fish for your fish stock. Ensure it is well rinsed and no blood is present.

The ratio of bones to mirepoix is 3:1. The one thing you will leave out here is the carrots. Swap leek for carrots.

You will need:

Bones and cleaned fish heads

1 rib celery

1 small onion

1 leek (white part only)

1 bouquet garni (thyme, parsley, bay leaf)

½ cup white wine (optional, but recommended)

Spice of your choice (peppercorns or other whole seed)

Cool water to cover

Sweat your fish bones in a hot dry sauté pan for a few minutes, then add all ingredients to the pot. Cover with water. Bring just to a boil, then reduce heat to a simmer. Cook for 40 minutes. Strain. Jar. Let cool before storing.

If you make fish stock, you can also prepare a *velouté*, which is a "mother sauce" in French cuisine.

ᴁ Velouté Sauce

Velouté is prepared by thickening your fish stock with a roux of flour and butter. It is a velvety addition to your table when served with any seafood. Velouté is also the jumping-off point for other sauces like Bercy that include finely chopped shallots and white wine. Flavor your velouté any way you wish with herbs, minced garlic, chives, parsley, chervil, or whatever else floats your boat.

You will need:

    1¾ cup fish stock

    2 tablespoons unsalted butter

    2 tablespoons all-purpose flour

Preheat your prepared fish stock in a pot on medium heat.

In a separate sauté pan, melt the butter on medium heat. Sprinkle the flour into the butter. Stir vigorously until fully incorporated and the roux begins to turn a slightly darker yellow. Slowly drizzle in the warm fish stock and whisk well.

Note: If you want to add shallots, garlic, or other additions of your choice, combine them at the melted butter stage, cooking until translucent.

Sauces made with a roux, like velouté or béchamel, can impart a slightly floury taste unless the sauce is simmered for a good 10–15 minutes after mixing. Take the time to let the flour be fully absorbed. Stir frequently to avoid a skin forming on top.

ᴁ Bone Broth

Bone broth is a trendy item these days. It is a broth of bones and veggies with the addition of an acid, like cider vinegar or white wine, that more quickly draws out the collagen and gelatin. Follow the beef stock recipe and add ¼–½ cup of wine or apple cider vinegar. Allow it to come to a low boil. Simmer for two hours. Skim, strain, and jar.

≈ Consommé

Now let's go on another journey to up your game with consommé. Boring old consommé, you say? *Au contraire*. Consommé is the epitome of sophistication in soups: the winnowing down of ingredients to a clear, clean, full flavor.

You start with your homemade stock, then proceed through an intricate procedure to remove the fats and impurities as you render it down to a distillate.

Growing up in my household, we were served consommé whenever we were sick. It was always the gentle reintroduction to digestive function following a stomach flu. It signaled the road to recovery. Today, a bowl of consommé is more likely a luxurious pool for a small parcel of veggies or quenelle of lobster to bathe in at a fine restaurant.

To make consommé, clarify your stock with a filter of ingredients called a raft. It's quite an operation, but when complete, the result is nothing like those cans of consommé we were served on our sick beds as children. It is an elegant, intense, and clear soup with exquisite mouthfeel. Savor slowly.

The Raft

The raft is a floating platform of egg white, lean ground meat, and white mirepoix (leave out the carrot) that attracts all the fats. It's about as gross looking as the scum in a polluted river, but that is exactly its purpose, because it is gathering everything you don't want from the stock. The proteins in the egg and meat draw out the proteins in the stock, clarifying it to an exquisite amber that is lively with subtle flavor.

It seems like a lot of work for a clarified consommé, and it is, but when you prepare a consommé, you are entering the realm of refinement.

Preparation

Whisk 3 egg whites, mirepoix, and lean ground meat together. You'll need enough meat and mirepoix so that a layer at least 1 inch thick floats above the broth. Add to pot and pour in cold stock. Bring to a boil while stirring. Turn down the heat and simmer for 45 minutes. The raft will rise to the top. As it sets, without disturbing the raft too much, gently make a hole in the center and carefully ladle out the consommé. Strain if any ingredients penetrate the clear liquid.

Serve in a small bowl as a starter, as a palate cleanser between rich dishes, or with a morsel of seafood, wisp of julienned vegetables, enoki mushrooms, white asparagus, handmade ravioli, or appetizer of your choice.

Consommé is neither trite nor a bowl of nothingness. It holds the spirit of all the ingredients that have passed through it. Make some, play around with ingredients in the raft too—use fish, mushrooms, meat, peppercorn—and develop your palate. Launch yourself into the culinary adventure.

Bon appétit.

Beyond the Maibowle: Sweet Woodruff in History and in the Kitchen

✺ Linda Raedisch ✺

Though I was more or less aware of sweet woodruff as a ground cover, I didn't get up close and personal with it until the early 2000s when I was working on my first book, *Night of the Witches*, about the celebration of Walpurgis Night. I'd kept my eyes peeled for what was blooming and budding around April 30 so I would know what materials would be available for the crafts and recipes I wanted to include, and I was sure to sneak a reference to my favorite tree—the beech—onto the first page. But I live in New Jersey, and sweet woodruff, *Galium odoratum*, whose dried leaves flavor the traditional German *Maibowle*, or May

wine punch, is a Eurasian native, which is why I didn't see it during my woodsy spring walks.

Sweet woodruff does, however, have some American cousins. With its crown of tiny, white, star-shaped flowers and slender, pointed leaves occurring in sixes at well-spaced intervals along the stem, shining bedstraw (*Galium concinnum*) resembles sweet woodruff most closely, but the rougher-looking cleavers (*Galium aparine*) is the only one, as far as I can tell, that has ever been consumed. In the early twentieth century, the Penobscot, Meskwaki, and Ojibwe were still steeping the leaves of cleavers, mixed with other herbs, for tea. (You may have found the seed husks of cleavers' bristly seeds "cleaving" to your pant legs after a walk in the woods.)

Because it takes me at least a year to write a book, I often find myself doing things out of season. I once made a gingerbread house in March, and I served my first batch of *sima*, a mildly alcoholic Finnish May Day drink, on Thanksgiving. When I realized I would need some sweet woodruff to make the traditional *Maibowle* for *Night of the Witches*, it was winter, and the only way to get fresh sweet woodruff was to order young, live plants through the mail, which I then dried for a few days before soaking in the wine.

How to describe the scent of dried sweet woodruff? Sweet. Heady. Woodsy. It also puts me in mind of the cigarette-rolling machine my parents used to bring out at family gatherings in the seventies. Sweet woodruff and tobacco aren't closely related, but I recently learned that coumarin, the chemical responsible for sweet woodruff's scent, is sometimes added to tobacco.

This spring, I decided to revisit the subject of sweet woodruff, but because procrastination is the mother of creativity (if not of good gardening), by the time I got around to proposing the article to my editor, the window for harvesting the plant had closed. This time, I cut to the chase, ordered an ounce of dried sweet woodruff through the mail, and emailed my German cousin-in-law, a yoga teacher and sporadic gardener, who confirmed that *Waldmeister*—"master of the forest," as it's known in German—must be harvested in April, before it blooms; after the flowers appear, it is "almost poisonous." She also told me that of her four children, only two liked the taste of sweet woodruff, and only in fizzy lemonade, not in the Jell-O–like *Wackelpudding* you can make at home from a mix. She herself dislikes the taste but loves the scent. (To me, the taste is a diluted form of the scent and needs sugar to bring it out.)

Cooking with Sweet Woodruff

My cousin-in-law and her kids notwithstanding, sweet woodruff had long been a popular ingredient in German soft drinks, desserts, and candies. No longer. Because of its high coumarin content, which could be harmful to children who eat too much of it, any child-friendly treat claiming *Waldmeister Geschmack*, "sweet woodruff flavor," is now artificially flavored—and artificially colored a bright emerald green. But when it comes to sweet woodruff's potentially poisonous properties, there's a loophole: the effects of the coumarin are minimized when taken with alcohol. That's why it's so often used to flavor alcoholic drinks like *Berliner Weisse* (a sour beer sweetened with fruit or sweet woodruff syrup), *Radler* (equal parts beer and fruit juice or soda), as well as the famous *Maibowle. Bowle*, a cognate of the English "bowl," is only used in reference to cold punch. It can mean either the punch or the bowl it's served in.

The aforementioned drinks are all German institutions, but the May wine capital of the world is the city of Arlon, Belgium, where it is known by the name of *Maitrank*, which means "May drink," in the Germanic language Francique-Moselle or "Moselle Franconian," after the river Mosel. Franconian is a descendant of the Frankish spoken by such luminaries as Charlemagne and a ninth-century monk named Wandalbert who plied his quill in the German abbey of Prüm, close to what is now the Belgian border but in those days was the Holy Roman Empire. In 854, Brother Wandalbert was the first to leave behind a written reference to Maitrank. More than a thousand years later, the city of Arlon would have cause to thank him for this.

Everyone agrees that sweet woodruff must be harvested before it blooms, which is usually by the end of April. Any later and it will have lost some of its fragrance and also be potentially toxic. I'm sure there's a scientific reason for this, but I prefer the folkloric one: that broomstick-riding witches spoil the plants when they fly over the forest on Walpurgis Night (April 30).

Meanwhile, in English-speaking lands, sweet woodruff never achieved the seasonal rock-star status that it continues to enjoy on the Continent. One of the first mentions of sweet woodruff in the English language comes from tenth-century Anglo-Saxon abbot Ælfric, who mentions it in his *Glossary*. "Woodruff" comes from Old English *wuderofe*, *wude* meaning "wood" and *rofe* meaning . . . well, no one's sure, but it may have referred to the plant's tendency to rove or wander—one of the reasons it makes such a good ground cover. The medieval English used it as a strewing herb, and sixteenth-century herbalist and Jesuit priest John Gerard observed that garlands of it were hung in bunches to sweeten the air.

Sweet woodruff in French is *aspérule*, from the plant's name in Latin, and, though it's been reclassified as *Galium odoratum*, it's still often referred to by its old binomial classification, *Asperula odorata*. *Galium*, like "galaxy," comes from the Greek word for "milk," and though the springtime carpet of sweet woodruff with its white, star-shaped flowers has been compared to the Milky Way, the name was probably chosen because some members of the genus *Galium* were used to curdle milk.

Brother Wandalbert was so taken with sweet woodruff that he gave it the epithet "Queen of the Meadows"—the German forest master's wife, perhaps? In Wandalbert's day, wine infused with sweet woodruff was drunk as a tonic to cleanse the body of poisons accumulated over the winter. The monks of Prüm served this medicinal punch to wayfarers and pilgrims who came to sneak a peek at the abbey's prize relic, a pair of Jesus's sandals. Prüm was eventually eclipsed by the nearby abbey of Trier (*they* had Jesus's robe), but Maitrank was never completely forgotten, keeping a low profile until the 1950s, when Arlonais doctor André Arend discovered Wandalbert's recipe and started making it himself, with the addition of cognac and fresh orange slices. The new old punch took off, and in May 1955, the city of Arlon celebrated its first annual Maitrank Festival. There is even a Royal Brotherhood of Maitrank of Arlon, a philanthropic organization that promotes the tradition and makes sure the punch is properly prepared. Their symbol is a yellow nymph, her body entwined with sweet woodruff, holding a bowl aloft. Their motto? "I like Maitrank."

Maitrank differs from the German Maibowle in a few important ways. For Maibowle, the sweet woodruff is macerated in riesling, a sweet white Rhine wine; for Maibowle, it's elbling, a dry white Mosel wine. Maibowle has strawberries floating in it; Maitrank has orange slices. Maitrank often has cognac in it and, depending on who's preparing it, may also contain port, Cointreau, lemon, black currant leaves, and even cinnamon.

For the citizens of Arlon, Maitrank is a sacred thing, so you might expect the Brotherhood to be highly secretive about its preparation. On the contrary, they've included a recipe on their website. When it comes to the best spots to gather the sweet woodruff, however, they will say only that it does best in shady beech groves.

May Wine Parfait

This recipe cleaves to the Maibowle tradition, though the orange zest in the cake base is a nod to the good folk of Arlon. If you like, you can swap the strawberries for mandarin oranges and replace the vanilla extract with a dash of cognac, but if you replace the riesling with elbling, you will need to add 2 tablespoons of sugar to the gelatin. Note that you'll need to begin soaking the woodruff in wine a day before you assemble the parfait.

If you're pregnant or breastfeeding, hold off on this recipe until the kids are a little older.

For the gelatin:

    2 cups riesling

    2 tablespoons dried sweet woodruff

    2 cups white grape juice

4 envelopes (¼ oz. each) Knox Unflavored Gelatine

13 × 9-inch baking pan

For the cake:

¾ cup butter, softened

1¼ cup sugar

2 eggs, beaten

¼ teaspoon vanilla extract

Zest of 1 small orange

1 cup flour, plus 1 cup

1½ teaspoons baking powder

½ cup milk

2 layer cake pans

16 oz. small, fresh strawberries

10–12 wine or parfait glasses or, in a pinch, glass ice cream bowls

Whipped cream to top

A day ahead, pour 2 cups riesling in a large jar. Add the dried sweet woodruff, screw on the lid, and swirl. Refrigerate overnight, swirling jar occasionally.

The next day, pour the wine in which the sweet woodruff has been macerating through a sieve into a large bowl, tilting the sieve so all the wine runs into the bowl. (There will still be tiny bits of sweet woodruff in the wine. This is fine.)

Pour 1 cup of the wine and 2 cups of white grape juice into a pot and heat to boiling. While it's heating, sprinkle—don't dump!—the 4 envelopes of gelatin over the remaining cold wine in the bowl. When the wine-juice mixture comes to a gentle boil, add it to the wine-gelatin mixture in the bowl, stirring until all the gelatin is dissolved, at least 5 minutes. Pour the liquid into the baking pan and chill for at least 3 hours.

In a large bowl, cream the butter and sugar together. Add eggs, vanilla extract, and orange zest. Mix 1 cup flour with baking powder and add it to the bowl. Mix well. Add milk and the rest of the flour. Stir until smooth. Pour into the greased and floured layer cake pans. Put them in a cold oven, turn the oven to 375°F, and bake for 25 minutes or until the top is lightly browned and a knife inserted in the center comes out clean. Let them cool for 10 minutes. Turn the cakes out onto a cutting board and cool further. When they're cool, use a parfait or wine glass to cut each into circles. Depending on the size of your glass, you should be able to make 5–6 circles per cake. Push 1 circle of cake into the bottom of each glass.

Cut the strawberries into halves or quarters and distribute them among the glasses.

When gelatin has set, cut into 1-inch squares and distribute equally among the glasses. Top with whipped cream just before serving. Serves 10–12.

Resources

Erichsen-Brown, Charlotte. *Medicinal and Other Uses of North American Plants*. New York: Dover, 1979.

Raedisch, Linda. *Night of the Witches: Folklore, Traditions, and Recipes for Celebrating Walpurgis Night*. Woodbury, MN: Llewellyn Publications, 2011.

La Royale Confrérie du Maitrank d'Arlon. "L'histoire de l'apéritif." Accessed September 9, 2021. https://royale-confrerie-maitrank .be/le-maitrank/.

Seasonings of the American South

⤳ Mireille Blacke ⤳

Upon completing my dietetic internship in 2011, I rewarded myself by adopting a hybrid rescue cat (a marble Bengal to be exact) with vibrant green eyes and ginger coloring, somewhat improbably (but aptly) named Cayenne. In addition to the typical Bengal agility, hyperactivity, and intelligence, Cayenne has much of the fire and spicy qualities associated with the pepper for which he is named. Appropriately, he has also been for me, at times, an unpredictable handful, a stomach irritant, a metabolic booster (Bengals need exercise!), and a mood enhancer. Also like a Bengal cat, a spice like cayenne is not suited for everyone. Our home expanded by welcoming Bengal

brother Cajun from the same hybrid cat rescue the following year, but my palate refused to do the same, continuing to avoid the more seasoned cuisine from the American South. To Southern locals, my choices were relatively tame. My stomach just couldn't make that Bengal-like leap into those flavors, or so I thought.

Though I'm completely in love with the music, architecture, and overall culture of New Orleans, I freely admit I'm a culinary coward when it comes to spicy food and generally won't indulge in some of the more popular dishes found in New Orleans and many other well-known cities of the American South. When visiting, I'd always ask my servers or hosts about the strength of the seasonings commonly found in particular dishes and was usually told, "Oh, that's mild." I'd further clarify with, "I'm from Connecticut . . . so, really, how spicy is it?" and then, with a slow grin, they'd usually advise me to order something else.

While Cayenne was teaching me a great deal about becoming a Bengal owner during that first year, I also realized I had quite a bit to learn about the origins of my favorite city's foods and the cuisine of the American South. I was a dietitian, after all, so I had zero excuses when it came to researching food and nutrition facts and fallacies!

For example, it's true that fresh cayenne peppers are the preferred hot capsicum in the American South, a key ingredient in hot and spicy dishes, and the thin, long, hot pepper in its ground form is a common ingredient in Cajun dishes in particular. It's also true that this ground powder adds reddish-brown color and fiery heat to sauces, soups, and stews. However, it's a common misperception that foods of the American

South are all hot and spicy. In fact, the seasonings known as the "Cajun Holy Trinity" are bell pepper (red and green), celery, and onion. The generous and creative use of the Cajun Holy Trinity leads to well-seasoned, distinctive, and highly flavored but not necessarily eye-watering, face-melting spicy foods.

Onions can be toxic or deadly for pets and other animals, so don't feed your pets foods or leftovers containing them.

Southern Seasoning Basics

The seasonings of the American South complemented cuisine of a people who demonstrated thriftiness with food preparation, had innovative skill in the kitchen, and made use of readily available ingredients out of necessity. For pioneering cooks in the American South, food was not to be wasted, and the ability to economize was imperative. The most important elements were freshness, adapting to circumstances and evolving accordingly, and "making do" with the ingredients at hand. Bold seasonings enhanced the flavors of the simplest foods, multiplied culinary options, extended the shelf life of foods, and in some cases, improved food safety.

Seasonings of the American South reflect a convergence of French, Spanish, Choctaw, and African influences. The French impressed the cooks of the American South with the strong sense of culinary economy or thriftiness regarding food and making the most with what one has. From the Spanish came a preference for spiced ("hot") foods and techniques involving mixing different protein sources (e.g., game, poultry, fish, etc.) and serving the mixture as a stew or accompanied by rice. The Choctaw Indian and African cultural influences upon the American South are directly responsible for impacting not only seasonings of the region, but arguably the most classic, emblematic dish of the American South as a whole: gumbo. Gumbo, a hearty, thick stew, reflects the blending of diverse traditions at the foundation of American Southern cooking, writes Terry Thompson-Anderson in *Cajun-Creole Cooking*.

It's said that the most critical "ingredient" to any successful gumbo is its *roux* (pronounced "roo"), usually formed by cooking a mixture of flour and butter (or oil). When it comes to thickening agents in gumbo recipes, *filé* powder and okra are the most referenced. Filé is made from dried and powdered sassafras leaves and was introduced to French immigrants (Creoles) in the New Orleans area by the Choctaw Indians, natives of the American South for hundreds of years, and masters in the culinary use of herbs and spices, notes restaurateur and baker Rebecca Rather. Introduced to the American South by African slaves, okra is a green pod vegetable that has shown its value as both a thickening agent in gumbo and as a side dish. African traditions influenced American Southern cuisine by incorporating the African technique of blending herbs and greens and via the use of slow cooking in iron pots, in which gumbo and other stews were patiently prepared, according to Thompson-Anderson.

For reference purposes, the following chart summarizes common seasonings of the American South and the dishes most prepared with each.

Seasoning	Southern Specialties
Bay Leaf	Beans, gumbo, marinades, meats, rice, sauces, seafood, soups, stews
Bell Pepper (Green, Red)	Gumbo, meat, salad, soups, stuffed peppers, sautés, stir-fries
Black Pepper	All fish, game, meat, poultry; all vegetables; beans, sauces, soups
Cayenne Pepper	Casseroles, dips, eggs, gumbo, meat, poultry, sauces, seafood, soups, vegetables; blended with chocolate
Celery	Gumbo, mirepoix, soups, stir-fries; seeds as dried spice in dips, marinades, pickling, sauces
Chicory	Beverages (café au lait), grains (risotto), pulses, quiche, salads, slaw
Cinnamon	Beverages, baked goods (bread pudding), cooked fruits, pickling, puddings, sauces, stews, sweets
Clove	Baked goods, beverages, carrots, chili, ham, marinades, pickling, sweet potatoes
Fennel Seeds (Whole)	Apple pies, beverages, bread, breath freshener, chicken, marinades, seafood (oysters Rockefeller), soups, spaghetti sauce, sweet pickles

Seasoning	Southern Specialties
Garlic	Mayo (aioli), meat (prime rib), poultry, salads, sauces, seafood (crawfish), soups, vegetables (cauliflower)
Ginger	Baked goods, cauliflower, drinks, fruits, marinades, meats, pancakes, pickling, poultry, preserves
Molasses	Baked goods (hermits/ gingersnaps/brown bread), beans, glazes, spare ribs
Mustard Seed	Almost every vegetable (mashed potatoes, roasted cauliflower), biscuits, cheese dishes, most meats/fish, peach chutney, relishes, sauces, salads
Onion	Beans, casseroles, dips, gumbo, maque choux, mirepoix, soups
Paprika	Deviled eggs, fish, goulash, meat, poultry, seafood, stews, vegetables
Parsley (Flat-Leaf)	On/over all vegetables, rice; cheese, chicken, eggs, fish, roasted lamb, salads, soups, steak, stuffing
Red Pepper Flakes	Jellies, pasta, pizza, sautéed greens, seafood
Sassafras Leaves	Beverages (root beer, tea), filé powder, hard candy
Thyme	Beans, cheese, eggs, lamb, meat, onions, pork, poultry, seafood, soups, stews, tomatoes, vegetables

As this table indicates, it doesn't take an excessive amount of seasonings to deliver a broad spectrum of flavor, and the average person doesn't need to be a master chef to incorporate Southern seasonings into their regular menu.

Ten Practical Spice Tips

1. Tolerance for spice and heat varies, and cayenne is no exception. Add cayenne to your recipes gradually when cooking (a pinch at a time) to avoid excessively hot (and painful) results.

2. When an onion is cut, enzymes at the cut area produce allicin, a sulfur-containing compound, resulting in burning and tearing eyes. To reduce eye irritation during slicing, cut onions under running water or submerged in water. Consider refrigerating the onion before cutting to slow the enzymatic reaction rate and also reduce irritation.

3. Chew a fresh parsley sprig after a garlicky meal to battle bad breath. Chewing fennel seeds after meals also freshens breath and aids digestion.

4. Adding potatoes or noodles will cool down a hot dish by spice absorption/neutralization. Milk or yogurt will also help cool a burning mouth. When cooking with cayenne specifically, avoid touching your skin, particularly your face, lips, and eyes.

5. Celery is an ingredient in mirepoix, a base for soups, stews, and stocks also consisting of diced carrots, onions, and sometimes parsnips. The cookbooks and websites in the reference lists at this article's end provide guidance on making mirepoix and other soups, stews, and stocks.

6. For a twist on breakfast, add ginger to your pancakes, or spice up your roasted carrots with ginger and orange zest. Note that ginger consumption in large quantities may lead to stomach distress and should be avoided by persons taking anticoagulants or with gallstones.

7. Caramelized onions are an optimal low-calorie flavor builder and alternative to traditional mayo and spreads. Add sweet, caramelized red onions to jazz up your grilled burgers, or use them as a condiment and sandwich topping.

8. To boost flavor, add mustard seed to mashed potatoes and roasted cauliflower.

9. Cinnamon is one of the most versatile pantry staples. Think about traditional and non-traditional uses for it: sweet potatoes, oatmeal, ground coffee, popcorn, pork chops and pork dishes, chili (or chili dogs), rice pilaf or couscous, and tea.

10. Regarding the most popular gumbo-thickening agents: Sprinkle filé powder sparingly and never add it while the gumbo is cooking because it will render the dish stringy and inedible, shares Rather. Thompson-Anderson notes that thyme compromises the flavor of filé powder. To counter one of the chief complaints about cooking with okra, char the okra pods first to prevent sliminess.

Recipes

❧ Creole Spice Blend
1 teaspoon fennel seed

1 teaspoon coriander seeds

1 teaspoon paprika

1 teaspoon whole black peppercorns

½ teaspoon whole white peppercorns

½ teaspoon cayenne pepper

1 teaspoon oregano, dried

Combine all the ingredients in a spice mill or small electric coffee grinder. Grind until smooth. Store in an air-tight container. Creative culinary minds will find numerous uses for this Creole spice blend, including the following recipe, which is one of the reasons I included it in this article.

༈ Creole Baked Beans

The following recipe is adapted from the Magnolia Grill of Durham, North Carolina, and incorporates the Cajun Holy Trinity (red bell pepper, onion, celery) into a versatile Creole dish. Feel free to substitute the chicken or lamb stock with a vegetarian or vegan substitute if that's your preference. Prep time for this recipe is 30 minutes, and cook time is 2 hours.

The night before you plan to cook your baked beans, prepare them for soaking. Pick through the dried beans, discarding any debris and beans that are shriveled or broken, and rinse in cold water. Place the beans in a bowl of water and soak overnight.

You will need:

1 pound small dried beans (red or white), soaked overnight

¼ cup olive oil

1 cup diced onion

2 ribs celery, cut into small dice

1 red bell pepper, cut into small dice

¼ cup minced garlic

1 bay leaf

1 teaspoon crushed red pepper flakes

1 tablespoon Creole spice blend (see pages 110–11)

3 tablespoons brown sugar

1 tablespoon dry mustard

1 cup tomatoes, seeded and chopped (or 1 can crushed tomatoes)

1 quart chicken stock or lamb stock (or vegetarian/vegan substitute)

Salt

2 tablespoons oregano, chopped

½ cup parsley

Cider vinegar to taste

Preheat oven to 300°F.

In a large, heavy, oven-safe pot, heat olive oil. Add the onion, celery, and pepper and cook until softened and lightly caramelized.

Add the garlic, bay leaf, red pepper flakes, and Creole spice blend. Cook for 2 minutes.

Drain the soaked beans and discard the liquid.

Stir in the brown sugar, mustard, tomatoes, drained beans, and enough chicken or lamb stock to cover by 1½ inches. Stir well and bring it to a boil on your stovetop. Remove the pan from the stovetop and tightly cover it with aluminum foil and a lid.

Transfer the pan to the oven and bake for 1½–2 hours. Check the liquid regularly and add more stock if necessary.

Cook until the beans are tender and most of the stock is absorbed. Season with salt to taste. Serves 6–8.

The flavor of these beans improves if they are cooked a day or two in advance and left to sit. Refrigerate them overnight or longer before serving.

✎ Maque Choux

I've adapted this heart-healthy recipe from *EatingWell* magazine for *maque choux* (pronounced "mock shoe"), a colorful Cajun corn and vegetable sauté, for nutrition education and cooking demos over the years. Here, extra-virgin olive oil replaces traditional bacon fat.

This recipe takes about 25 minutes to prepare and yields 6 servings.

You will need:

1 tablespoon extra-virgin olive oil

1 small onion, diced

½ medium red bell pepper, diced

2 cloves garlic, minced

3 cups corn (about 4 ears if cutting off the cob)

¼ cup water

1 medium tomato, chopped

3 scallions, sliced

½ teaspoon finely chopped fresh thyme, or ¼ teaspoon dried

½ teaspoon paprika

½ teaspoon salt

¼ teaspoon cayenne pepper, or to taste

Heat large nonstick skillet over medium heat and add the olive oil. Add onion and stir until it starts to soften, about 2 minutes. Add the bell pepper and garlic and stir for another 2 minutes. Add the corn and water and stir until it is tender but firm, about 5 minutes more. Remove the pan from heat and stir in the remaining ingredients. Serve hot or cooled.

⤜ Gumbo Ya Ya

One of the most popular brands of cayenne is Tabasco sauce, the nationally marketed liquid form of cayenne pepper grown on Avery Island, Louisiana. Some recipes (like this one) list Tabasco or cayenne specifically because even though they serve the same purpose, each reacts differently in the cooking process and different quantities are required. Visit the Tabasco brand's website for some recipes that incorporate Tabasco sauce, including several for deviled eggs; see the references section at the end of this article for that information.

This traditional Cajun recipe for gumbo, adapted from Sodexo Quality of Life Services, combines ingredients like chicken, smoked sausage, and okra, with cayenne pepper, Tabasco sauce, and fresh garlic. This recipe takes a little over 4 hours to prepare and serves 10 as a meal with rice.

You will need:

    2 cups canola oil

    1½ cups flour

    1 large yellow onion, diced

    2½ cups diced celery

    1 large red pepper, diced

    1 large green pepper, diced

2 cups okra

2½ quarts low-sodium chicken stock

4 teaspoons black pepper

1 tablespoon kosher salt

1 teaspoon dried thyme (or 1 tablespoon fresh)

1 teaspoon dried oregano (or 1 tablespoon finely chopped fresh)

½ teaspoon cayenne pepper

4 teaspoons Tabasco sauce

3 teaspoons fresh garlic, minced

2 bay leaves

1½ pounds chicken thigh meat, raw and cubed

1½ pounds smoked sausage, cut into half-moons

10 cups cooked white rice

baguette, sliced into ½-inch pieces

Whisk oil and flour over a medium heat in a heavy pot. Stir continuously until the mix becomes a dark copper-brown, about 45 minutes.

Add the onion, celery, peppers, and okra. Sauté for a minute or so, creating a large ball. Slowly whisk in the chicken stock until well incorporated. Add the spices and bring to a boil.

When the gumbo reaches a boil, add the chicken and sausage and simmer on low heat for 2½–3 hours.

Serve over rice and garnish with a slice of the baguette.

I adore my beloved Cayenne and his Bengal antics to this day, though he still has his "spicier" moments that wreak havoc on my nerves. My appreciation for him has grown over time, as has my love for the rich culture of the American South; I simply cannot imagine my life without either of them. Though I'm not able to visit this remarkable American region as often as I'd like, I have a better understanding of the spectrum of seasonings of Southern foods, and I certainly do appreciate their flavors, sounds, and sights in my own unique way. I'm happy to have shared those experiences in writing, and I encourage readers of this article to explore the cuisine of the American South for themselves. Any way you slice it, that's fine by me.

Resources

Angers, W. Thomas. *Cajun Cuisine: Authentic Cajun Recipes from Louisiana's Bayou Country*. Lafayette, LA: Beau Bayou Publishing Company, 1985.

Barker, Ben, and Karen Barker. *Not Afraid of Flavor: Recipes from Magnolia Grill*. Chapel Hill, NC: University of North Carolina Press, 2003.

Carey, Joseph. *Creole Nouvelle: Contemporary Creole Cookery*. Lanham, MD: Taylor Trade Publishing, 2004.

Macque Choux Recipe. *EatingWell*. July/August 2008. Accessed September 3, 2021. https://www.eatingwell.com /recipe/249731/macque-choux/.

National Onion Association. Accessed September 4, 2021. www .onions-usa.org.

Rather, Rebecca. *Pastry Queen Parties: Entertaining Friends and Family, Texas Style*. New York: Ten Speed Press, 2009.

Sodexo Quality of Life Services. "Gumbo Ya Ya." Accessed September 3, 2021. https://loveoffood.sodexo.com/recipe/gumbo-ya-ya/.

Thompson-Anderson, Terry. *Cajun-Creole Cooking*. Fredericksburg, TX: Shearer Publishing, 2003.

Further Reading

Fitzmorris, Tom. *New Orleans Food: More than 225 of the City's Best Recipes to Cook at Home*. New York: Stewart, Tabori & Chang, 2006.

Oak Alley Plantation Restaurant and Inn. *Oak Alley Plantation Cooking*. Vacherie, LA: Oak Alley Plantation Restaurant and Inn, 2003.

Tabasco. "Deviled Eggs with Tabasco Original Red Sauce." Accessed September 12, 2021. https://www.tabasco.com/recipe/deviled-eggs-with-tabasco-original-red-sauce/.

What's Cooking America. "Creole Baked Beans." Accessed September 3, 2021. https://whatscookingamerica.net/vegetables/creole bakedbeans.htm.

Herbs for Stir-Fries

☙ Elizabeth Barrette ❧

Stir-fries are delicious and healthy if made with those goals in mind. Herbs and spices greatly contribute to the flavor and also the nutrition. You can combine herbs with a particular goal, such as digestion, in stir-fries just as you would in stew or tea. To get the best results, you need to know not only which herbs work best in stir-fries, but what stage to add them based on their qualities.

Creating Tasty Stir-Fries

It is not difficult to make good stir-fries once you know how, but it can be tricky in ways that aren't obvious. My partner and I had an opportunity to get a bargain wok, so we decided to make an adventure of learning how to

use it. What I learned, very quickly, is that most stir-fry recipes are *terrible*. They misuse ingredients, list steps out of logical order, and produce discouraging outcomes. You can follow a bad recipe exactly and get a wretched stir-fry as a result. So read carefully, and if something sounds stupid, it probably is.

Another problem is that restaurant stir-fries, while tasty enough to enjoy, are often just as badly designed. So you are often better off understanding your ingredients and how the stir-fry process works, then just making your own. If you are a decent cook with a good grasp of ingredients, you will probably make better stir-fries than most restaurants; if you are a fan of herbs enough to know the nuances of their use, you can make *much* better stir-fries at home.

You can make a stir-fry in any cuisine. Just look at what fats, herbs, produce, and proteins it uses and then put them together in a wok or skillet. Don't be afraid to try new things. If you're not making any mistakes, you're not learning, you're coasting. New foods can be exciting, especially in stir-fries.

Preparation

Making a stir-fry takes me about an hour, start to finish, with an assistant. Precut, canned, or otherwise prepared ingredients make it go faster. Look at recipe times, practice, and you'll learn how long it takes for you.

Prep all your ingredients in advance. You won't have time to prep and stir-fry at the same time, because once you put anything in the pan, you must keep it moving. An assistant is extremely helpful but not required. Cut all the ingredients small and thin, as close to the same size as possible. This makes them cook faster.

Use the best, freshest ingredients you can get. Stir-fries are scrumptious and nutritious if you use good fruits, vegetables, and lean meats or tofu. They're not nearly as fun if the ingredients are poor. A good rule of thumb is to use two to four different types of produce in a mixed stir-fry. You might want more in a vegetarian one or fewer for a meat one.

Cooking

A wok works better than a skillet, but you can stir-fry in a skillet just fine. Use what you have and enjoy cooking with.

You need a cooking fat with a high smokepoint. Ghee (clarified butter) is all but impossible to burn at ordinary cooking temperatures. Other popular choices include almond oil, grape seed oil, and sunflower oil. Some only work if *refined:* avocado oil, olive oil, palm oil, and peanut oil. Sesame oil has a wonderful nutty, roasty flavor but only when used in the sauce; if poured on as a top dressing it can be overpowering and tastes almost burnt. It needs to cook into the dish for a couple of minutes.

When seasoning, don't overuse salt or salty ingredients. One of the biggest flaws I found in stir-fry recipes was drowning everything in soy sauce until that's all you can taste. If you wouldn't use a quarter-cup of Worcestershire sauce, don't use that much soy sauce. A teaspoon to a tablespoon is plenty. Let the herbs and vegetables shine on their own. The same goes for sugary things like mirin or molasses: less is more. Stir-fries are healthy unless you add lots of bad ingredients.

Add ingredients to the pan in order of cooking time. Tougher things like onions go in before softer things like peapods. Things that only need to be heated through (like canned water chestnuts) or wilted (like fresh leafy herbs) go in just before you add the sauce.

Texture is a matter of personal preference. Some people like their vegetables crunchy, some *al dente*, and others silky-soft. Don't let anyone "should" on you. Cook it however you like it. Most meats (chicken, pork, seafood), however, should be cooked until done. A few (beef, lamb) may be safely served rare. That can be a difference of much less than a minute when you are cooking tiny slivers in a very hot pan. Use the edge of your spatula to cut a piece in half and look at its inside if you're not sure. A thermometer won't work on pieces that small, and timing is only an estimate.

Some stir-fries are intended as a separate main dish or side dish. Most are meant to be served over a starch such as brown rice or noodles. That soaks up the delicious sauce and keeps you feeling full for longer.

Aromatics

Aromatics are herbs, spices, and occasionally vegetables that have intense flavor and aroma. A stir-fry customarily begins by heating fat in a hot pan, then sautéing some aromatics before the other ingredients get added. These aromatics tend to consist of seeds, bark, hard roots, or other tough plant parts that benefit from lots of cooking. They are typically used whole at this stage. The longer cooking time will eventually soften and break down some of them. For things that won't break down at all, like a cinnamon stick, try to find and remove them before serving. If people don't like biting into the smaller ones, such as whole peppercorns, most can be cracked down to smaller size.

Be aware that some herbs and spices, as well as things that are usually considered vegetables, can behave very differently when sautéed as aromatics. Ginger alone is intensely hot; garlic alone is intensely pungent; but sauté them together and both become much mellower and more complex. Carrots and celery used as aromatics put most of their flavor into the oil, so their taste and texture differ from when they are used as vegetables. Onions get a lot mellower too, so if you want them for punch, cut some more finely and add those later.

Furthermore, some herbs and spices come in multiple forms, such as cilantro (leaf) and coriander (seed). These complement each other when used in the same dish. However, they typically benefit from being added at different times due to their different qualities. This is a natural application in stir-fry with its staged preparation.

Start your stir-fry with about 2 tablespoons of heat-resistant oil and 2 to 4 aromatics. The quantities vary a lot—you can use ½ onion sliced into crescents, 3 juniper berries is plenty, and people will argue over whether to throw in 1 dried chili pepper or 5. Look at various recipes for inspiration, think about what you like, and add the strongest ingredients more sparingly than milder ones. Here are some aromatics you might like to try:

Ajwain: A tiny seed-like fruit with a pungent, bitter, and herbal flavor. It is related to caraway and fennel. The flavor has been compared to anise, oregano, and thyme. Ajwain appears in Indian recipes.

Allspice Berries: Round, hard, dark brown, dried berries. Their name comes because they taste like a combination of cinnamon, clove, and nutmeg. They're great for sweet or warming stir-fries.

Bell Pepper: Mildly spicy, juicy and crunchy when fresh, large hollow fruits. They come in a rainbow of colors, and while this fades a little when cooked, a mix of bell pepper colors looks splendid in stir-fries.

Caraway Seeds: Tiny curved fruits from the carrot family, they have a fennel-like flavor.

Cardamom Pods/Seeds: Triangular pods with tiny seeds that have a sweet, floral, faintly spicy flavor. Popular in Indian and Middle Eastern cuisines.

Carrot: A sweet, crunchy root. Purple carrots are more prone to a stronger peppery flavor that works well as an aromatic.

Celeriac: Celery root, hard with a strong celery flavor. It is widely used in Mediterranean and Northern European cuisines.

Celery: The crescent-shaped stalk of the celery herb, crunchy and juicy with a fresh green flavor. It is key in Cajun and Creole cuisines.

Chili Pepper: Hot, spicy versions of a hollow fruit, available in many colors, shapes, and intensities. Different cuisines use different cultivars, so try to match them.

Cinnamon: Reddish-brown rolled bark or powder with a sweet-hot flavor. Goes with other warming spices like clove and allspice.

Clove: Reddish-brown pegs with a sweet-hot flavor. They blend well with other warming spices like cinnamon and allspice.

Coriander Seeds: The hard round seeds of the cilantro plant, tangy and citrusy. Often used with cilantro leaves.

Cumin Seeds: Tiny curved seeds with an herbal-peppery flavor. They form the base of many spice blends.

Fennel: Tiny curved seeds and large white root that both have a strong licorice flavor. It is common in Middle Eastern and Indian cuisines.

Fenugreek Seeds: Tiny round seeds with a bittersweet flavor. They are used in Indian, Middle Eastern, and North African cuisines.

Garlic: Small white bulb that breaks into cloves, pungent and musky. It's often combined with ginger.

Ginger: Branching yellow root with intensely hot flavor. It's often combined with garlic.

Grains of Paradise: Tiny dark seeds of *Aframomum melegueta* with a floral, peppery flavor. Ideal for subtle nuances. Important in some African cuisines.

Juniper Berries: Small, dark, dried berries of the juniper tree with a strong piney, resinous flavor. Good for cutting through fat, stands up to dark meats. Key to Turtle Island (native North American) cuisines.

Leek: Like a giant green onion with a mellow pungent flavor. Ideal in delicate recipes to avoid overpowering other flavors. Important to some milder European cuisines.

Lemongrass: A giant tropical grass with thickened base stems and a vivid citrusy flavor. Great top note for stir-fries. Key to some South Asian cuisines.

Mustard Seeds: Small round seeds with a hot-tangy flavor; can be yellow, brown, or black. Used in Indian and nearby cuisines.

Nigella Seeds: Tiny black seeds with herbaceous and oniony notes. Popular in Indian, Middle Eastern, and North African cuisines.

Onion: Large round bulb with hot pungent taste. Used in most stir-fries, it adds a lot of fiber as well as flavor.

Peppercorns: Small, hard dried fruits with a hot, spicy taste. Most cuisines use these. Very versatile.

Sage: Leathery gray-green leaves with a musky, resinous taste. Excellent with dark meats and robust flavors. Key to Turtle Island (native North American) cuisines.

Scallion: Young onion with narrow white base and long green leaves and milder than the big kind. Ubiquitous in Asian cuisines.

Star Anise: Star-shaped seedpods with a powerful licorice flavor. Used in some Asian cuisines.

Tomato: A usually red, fragrant, juicy vegetable. Use minced dried tomatoes or a dab of paste to make a red stir-fry. Widely used in Mediterranean and American cuisines.

Some combinations of aromatics are traditional within particular cultures or cuisines. These are well proven to work, even if you use them elsewhere.

African: Cinnamon, cumin, grains of paradise, and either ginger or chilies in olive oil (North Africa), peanut oil (East Africa), or red palm oil (West Africa).

Asian Trinity: Garlic, ginger, and scallions in peanut, coconut, or rice bran oil.

Australian Citrusy Blend: Finger lime (*Citrus australasica*), lemon myrtle (*Backhousia citriodora*), and Australian native ginger (*Alpinia caerulea*) in sunflower or olive oil.

Cajun / Creole Holy Trinity: Celery, green bell peppers, and onions in sunflower or olive oil.

French Mirepoix: Carrots, celery, onions / leeks in olive oil.

Hispanic Sofrito: Garlic, onions, tomato (sometimes bell peppers) in olive oil.

Indian: Chilies, ginger, onions (and often cumin, coriander, cardamom pods) in ghee or coconut oil.

Middle Eastern: Caraway, cumin, shallots, tomato in olive oil.

Thai Curry Combo: Chilies, garlic, lemongrass, shallots/onions in coconut oil.

Turtle Island Blend: Juniper berries and sage in sunflower oil.

Herbs as Vegetables

The middle part of a stir-fry includes adding all the main ingredients. Typically, the vegetables are cooked first, the firmer ones and then the softer ones. A space is cleared in the middle, then the meat or plant protein is cooked. Things that only need to heat through and leaves that only need to wilt are added toward the end.

There are many leafy green herbs that work well as vegetables in this stage of a stir-fry. Chives, cilantro, and flat parsley can be added in substantial quantities. Basil, mint, and oregano can be added more moderately. Celery leaves, dill, and Thai basil tend to be used sparingly.

Some plants, like bok choi, Swiss chard, and beet greens, have tough stalks with tender leaves. These should be separated, the stalks added first and the leaves later. That way both cook properly.

Sauces

A stir-fry usually has a sauce poured over it for the last few minutes. The base can be water or broth. Often it has oils, sweeteners, acids, condiments, thickeners, or spices added. At this stage, herbs or spices should be powdered, or fresh and minced, so they blend in better. Figure anywhere from a few tablespoons to half a cup of sauce, depending on amount of other foods.

Sweeteners such as honey, molasses, and maple syrup add texture as well as flavor. Mirin is a thick, syrupy rice wine that also adds savory notes.

Citrus is often added in the form of zest and juice. Lemon, lime, and orange are the most common. Lime is traditional with coconut in South Asian curries and Hispanic dishes. Any of the three can be used to make citrus chicken in Chinese cuisine.

Vinegar balances sweet ingredients. Rice vinegar is particular to Asian cuisine but works well in others too. Strong flavors like balsamic or apple cider vinegar can really punch up a stir-fry. For a pure sour flavor, however, use white vinegar. If you use a live-cultured vinegar and stir-fry very briefly after the sauce goes in, you gain the benefit of probiotics.

Thickeners make the sauce "set" when it hits the hot pan. I prefer cornstarch or tapioca starch; some other people use wheat flour instead. Once you pour in the sauce, you only need to stir-fry until it thickens, usually one to three minutes—unless you are steaming or doing something else with different timing.

Condiments offer a great way to add flavor in sauces. Consider barbecue sauce, fish sauce, horseradish, ketchup, mustard, oyster sauce (the real cooked-down kind), soy sauce, steak sauce, or Worcestershire sauce.

Dry spice blends can be turned into sauce by adding enough liquid to reach the desired consistency. Usually water or oil is used here. Allow time to soak for best results.

Pastes can be used to make sauces by thinning them with water, broth, oil, vinegar, or other liquids. Anchovy paste, curry paste, garlic-ginger paste, pesto, tomato paste, and wasabi all work well for this. So do most nut butters.

Tadkas

In addition to the water-based sauces used in most stir-fries, there's another trick from India called a *tadka*. This is an oil-based topping that adds intense impact, because fat carries flavor. Aromatics, usually whole, are sautéed in fat and then poured over the top of a dish. You can also use a tadka to season the cooked grains or other base that you are serving with your stir-fry. The key is to use herbs and spices whose flavors are oil-soluble. If an edible plant has a real essential oil associated with it, then it probably works in a tadka. Alliums and peppers are among the most popular but others include ajwain, black mustard seed, cinnamon sticks, cardamom pods, cumin seed, clove, fenugreek seed, ginger, nigella seed, and star anise. Minced dried tomato is particularly useful in using a tadka to flavor rice.

A tadka works much like sautéing aromatics at the beginning. Melt a few tablespoons of oil with a high smokepoint, such as ghee. Add several aromatic herbs and spices. For things that will actually cook, like alliums or ginger, sauté until they begin to brown and soften. These can be left in when you pour the tadka over the food. Whole hard spices should be sautéed until toasted and fragrant. These things, like a cinnamon stick, should be fished out with a slotted spoon before pouring the tadka. Another clue is color. Many aromatic herbs and spices convey intense color, so watch for things like dried hot peppers to dye the oil bright red as a sign that it's ready. If you use a strongly colored oil, like red palm oil, you'll have to compensate for not being able to see that.

Should you become fond of this method, you may wish to invest in a tadka pan, which is a tiny skillet often with a spout for pouring. In America, you may see it sold as an "egg skillet" or such. A gravy pot or butter warmer is similar but deeper and will also work.

Conclusion

Stir-fries make healthy and delicious meals. It's a great way to eat large amounts of fresh vegetables. It's also an opportunity to use up whatever you have; you can stir-fry almost anything, and combine small amounts of several things. Herbs and spices contribute to the intense flavors and colors for which some stir-fries are so famous. By using the herbs particular to a given area, you can recreate its cuisine in this format, even if the locals don't tend to stir-fry.

No-Cook Herby Marinades, Spreads, and Sauces

⌇ Annie Burdick ⌇

Herbs have proven themselves over and over again to be a staple for flavorful cooking. Marinara sauce without basil feels lackluster. Stuffing sans sage and thyme tastes less like Thanksgiving. A glorious, steaming dish of Thai food would feel incomplete without some fresh lemongrass or Thai basil in the mix.

The fact is, even when we don't realize they're there, herbs are shaping the way we react to and experience our meals. But something many herb-heavy recipes seem to share is a level of complexity. While adding fresh herbs to any meal is a great way to upgrade it, what about meals that are ultra simple and quick to make and have herbs at their core?

Sometimes there's a great appeal in enjoying a meal that required minimal time, effort, or even heat (especially in the warmer months). While you may have to do a bit of cooking the accompaniments for these recipes (whether grilling some meat or boiling some noodles), each sauce and marinade that follows is a no-cook starter for a delicious, flavorful meal—where your fresh herbs get to be the star of the show.

What Makes a Marinade?

Marinades are endlessly customizable, which is part of what makes them so fun, easy, and tasty to use in cooking. But, that doesn't mean there aren't some important elements every marinade needs. At its core, a good marinade needs at least three key elements: an acid, a fat, and some flavor. The acidic component helps tenderize the meat while it marinates, allowing all the flavors to penetrate and sink in. It's also part of balancing the flavor, not allowing the other elements to weigh it down or make it overly heavy. Meanwhile, the fat balances the acid, keeping it from making the flavor too tangy or sour. It also helps the meat retain moisture as it's cooking. And the flavor elements are self-explanatory; these are any add-ons that give the marinade its depth and deliciousness.

Traditional fat options include oils, coconut milk, or yogurt. Acids could be things like lemon or orange juice, vinegar, wine, or buttermilk. And flavor elements are fairly endless, but this is where your herbs come in! Try things like garlic, zests, soy sauce, sugar, honey, and so on.

✤ Creamy Lemon Dill Marinade
This marinade that tastes like (and is perfect for) a fresh summery evening is, like the rest, a breeze to put together. The

combination of fresh dill, lemon juice, and garlic is fragrant and totally irresistible. In the peak of summer it feels timely, but it's just as lovely throughout the rest of the year, conjuring those warm days with fresh flavor. The key to this one is that it's a blended marinade. Yes, you can make the same marinade without blending, but once blended it becomes a richer sauce that adheres much better to meat and veggies, so the taste sticks around more after cooking.

You will need:

    ½ cup Greek yogurt

    1 tablespoon garlic

    Juice of half a lemon

    1 teaspoon fresh dill

    1 tablespoon oil

    2 tablespoons water

    Sprinkle of red pepper flakes

Combine all ingredients in a food processor or blender and pulse until smooth and combined. This is the key to this marinade. Add the marinade to a bowl or bag with 1 pound of meat or vegetables. This is a perfect fresh chicken marinade, but it would also work well with fish, other poultry, or grilled veggies. Marinate for 1 hour, or several if possible, then cook up your main course of choice and enjoy an ultra-fresh, herby meal. Serve with some rice, couscous, roasted potatoes, salad, vegetables, or warm pita bread.

ᕲ Rich Rosemary Balsamic Marinade

The combination of several rich, earthy, intensely flavorful elements here creates an amazingly flavorful marinade that packs quite a punch of flavor, even after you prepare the meat or veggies you marinate. I think this marinade is particularly fantastic for steak of any sort, and I absolutely love using it for steak pieces. However, for vegetarians, it would make a great marinade for veggies like asparagus, zucchini, onions, mushrooms, or carrots, all of which could then be grilled or roasted.

You will need:

  1 tablespoon minced garlic

  1 tablespoon Worcestershire sauce

  2 teaspoons honey

  ⅓ cup balsamic vinegar

  ⅓ cup red wine (any kind—cheap works!)

  1 packed tablespoon roughly chopped fresh rosemary

Combine all ingredients in a plastic bag or bowl, then add 1 pound of meat or vegetables. Whatever you choose to use it for, marinate for at least 1 hour, several if possible. Transfer the meat or vegetables to a grill or pan and cook to your liking, then add a few spoonfuls of the marinade back to the pan at the last minute or two for an extra blast of rich, herby flavor.

Spreads

✎ Minty Fresh Whipped Feta Spread

A highly versatile spread that works as a sandwich topper, appetizer component, and sauce all in one? I'm here for it. The main element of this spread, the feta, adds a rich, tangy flavor no matter how you customize it. Fresh mint and parsley are great starting points for this spread, but getting creative with other herb combos or adding sun-dried tomatoes, roasted red peppers, or other additions is also super fun and produces great results.

You will need:

8 ounces feta (block or crumbles)

⅔ cup sour cream or Greek yogurt

3 ounces softened cream cheese

½ tablespoon garlic

2 teaspoons honey

1 tablespoon olive oil

2 tablespoons fresh parsley

1–2 tablespoons fresh mint

Salt and pepper to taste

Combine all ingredients in a food processor or blender and pulse until smooth and creamy. This is a very customizable spread; using mint and parsley is only a suggestion, as you could swap in most any herb you love with similarly delicious results and a new flavor blend. If the consistency isn't quite to your liking, add additional tablespoons of sour cream or Greek yogurt until it's nice and smooth.

Once you've got a lovely whipped consistency, it's ready to be used. The applications for this spread are endless, but here are a few possibilities to get your wheels turning:

• Toast slices of baguette and top with a spread of whipped feta, some crushed walnuts, and a drizzle of honey or balsamic glaze for a perfect appetizer.

- Fill a bowl with the spread, top with chopped artichokes, black olives, roasted red peppers, olive oil drizzle, or any other toppings of your choice, then serve as a dip with pita chips or toasted pita bread.

- Grill chicken breasts or thighs with seasoning or marinade of your choice, then spread some whipped feta on top before serving.

- Use it as an extra-flavorful spread on subs, sandwiches, and wraps.

➳ Cheddar and Chive Spread

This one comes directly from my grandma, who was an amazing cook and made the most heartwarming, soul-filling food. After she passed, my family compiled her infamous recipes into a little book, something I cherish using. This spread is the epitome of growing up in Wisconsin—plenty of cheese, beer, and savory flavor. But she knew what was up, and it also uses a nice hearty serving of fresh herbs in the form of chopped chives. It's great spread on crackers or pretzels but also works as a sandwich spread, if you really want to treat yourself.

You will need:

8 ounces cheddar cheese, shredded

¼ cup beer

2 tablespoons mayo

½ teaspoon prepared mustard

1 tablespoon chives, chopped

2 teaspoons pimientos

Mix all ingredients to combine.

Sauces

✎ *Basil Red Pepper Vegan Blender Sauce*

When I first made this sauce, I was completely blown away. Everything about it is amazing, from the fact that it takes all of two minutes to put together to the fact that it's vegan and tastes incredible. This will quickly become a staple for those who love pasta and simple, flavorful meals.

For the sauce:

½ cup cashews

⅔ cup roasted red peppers (from a jar; feel free to include some of the oil they're packed in too)

¼ cup fresh basil leaves

1 clove garlic

1–2 tablespoons olive oil (more if needed)

Salt and pepper to taste

For serving:

About 8 ounces of pasta (I love this on a thick noodle like tagliatelle or something sturdy like rigatoni)

Grated parmesan or vegan parmesan

Chopped parsley

Toasted breadcrumbs

Place all sauce ingredients in a blender cup and pulse until it forms a smooth sauce consistency. Add additional drizzles of olive oil if it's too thick. Cook the pasta to your liking and, while it's still warm, top with the sauce and optional additional toppings like sprinkles of cheese, breadcrumbs, and parsley.

These bonus ingredients add a great extra flavor, as well as some pleasant textural experiences.

⚵ *Sweet and Spicy Basil Pesto*

The pinnacle of a classic pesto usually involves a roster of simple and time-honored ingredients: basil, olive oil, nuts, and parmesan chief among them. But what if you want to fire up the flavor a bit more? I'd recommend this alternative, which takes into account all the classic ingredients but adds some spice with Calabrian chilies, sweetness with honey, and depth of flavor with balsamic vinegar and lemon juice.

You will need:

> 1 cup packed fresh basil leaves
>
> 4 jarred Calabrian chilies in oil (about 1 tablespoon of chilies)
>
> ¼ teaspoon lemon juice
>
> ¼ cup nuts of your choice (pine nuts are generally preferred)
>
> 1 teaspoon chopped garlic
>
> 2 tablespoons parmesan or preferred aged cheese
>
> 1 teaspoon spicy honey (or regular honey if you prefer it or can't find spicy)
>
> ⅓ cup olive oil
>
> Splash of balsamic vinegar
>
> Salt and pepper to taste

Combine all ingredients in a blender or food processor, pulsing until smooth and combined. If needed, add additional teaspoons of olive oil until achieving the desired consistency. Season to taste.

This pesto is great served so many ways—on top of pasta, meat, or veggies, as a starter. I also love it on top of some toasted baguette slices, with a bit of goat cheese and a drizzle of balsamic glaze. Store your homemade pesto in a jar in the fridge for about a week, or freeze it for up to a few months.

✿ Creamy Multipurpose Herby Sauce

This versatile sauce is not only packed with aromatic, delicious herbs, but it pairs nicely with so many meals. While it could be as simple as a dip for raw vegetables or pretzels at your next party, it's light and saucy enough to drizzle over roasted potatoes, steak, chicken, fish, and just about anything else you set your mind to.

You will need:
- ¾ cup Greek or plain yogurt
- ½ cup sour cream
- 2 tablespoons mayo
- 1 tablespoon dijon mustard
- 2 tablespoons chopped dill
- 2 tablespoons chopped chives
- ½ tablespoon chopped mint or parsley
- 2 tablespoons lemon juice
- 1 teaspoon red wine vinegar
- 1 teaspoon sugar
- 1 teaspoon olive oil
- Salt and pepper to taste

Combine and mix all ingredients together thoroughly. Refrigerate until just before using. Drizzle on top of meat or potatoes or dip away!

✎ Creamy Herb Dressing

This is another of my grandma's recipes that I remember fondly, and my family continued making the fantastic salad after she passed. Every element was excellent, but her home-made creamy, herby dressing (something she invented herself) was honestly the star of the show. This dressing will go great with so many salads, pasta salads, grains, or bowls.

You will need:

    1 clove garlic

    ¼ cup mayo

    ½ cup plain yogurt

    ¼ cup grated parmesan

    1 tablespoon liquid from a can of artichokes (substitute with olive oil and more herbs if you don't happen to be using artichokes for the salad)

    1 teaspoon fresh Italian herbs of your choice (oregano, parsley, and basil all work well)

Add garlic to a food processor and blend until finely minced. Add the rest of the ingredients and pulse on and off until smooth and combined.

Health
and
Beauty

Oh, My Aching Feet!

≈ JD Walker ≈

We demand so much from our feet every day. We stuff them into tight-fitting shoes. We stand on them too much—or not enough, so that they swell from the act of sitting all day.

Inadvertently sloshing through puddles and getting stubbed on the furniture in the middle of the night—it's tough to be a couple of lower extremities. Isn't it time to give your feet a little TLC?

You could treat yourself to a pedicure, but who has the time or the money? Why not make a date with your feet for a little spa treatment at home with a simple and soothing footbath?

Identifying the Problem

Any number of conditions can cause foot pain or discomfort, and many of them require the attention of a medical professional. Bone spurs, bursitis, corns, and gout, for example, are conditions that can be eased temporarily with a good soak but may require the help of a professional to diagnose the cause and eliminate the problem entirely.

Plantar fasciitis involves the inflammation of the ligament or fascia that attaches the heel to the toes on the bottom of the foot. It can be treated with rest, stretching, and footbaths but should probably be looked at by a healthcare professional if the condition persists for more than a few months.

Humans have almost 8,000 nerves in their feet, which is why the feet are often the most ticklish part of the body.

Those with diabetes know neuropathy is of special concern when it comes to their feet. Peripheral neuropathy causes numbness and tingling in the extremities. While this can be relieved in part with a warm water soak, care should be taken not to use water that is too hot. Diabetics should also be sure to carefully check their feet and legs for sores, infections, and a lack of feeling that should be addressed immediately by a professional.

However, if you simply have run-of-the-mill tired feet, a good soaking is just what you might need.

How Does It Work?

You might hear the argument that all you need is hot water to get the benefits of a footbath. It is true that soaking the feet in a container of water heated to around 104 degrees Fahrenheit is relaxing. The heated water helps bring blood flow to the extremities and relaxes tight muscles in the feet.

However, herbs and essential oils bring benefits of their own. The benefits of these products are easily absorbed through the feet because you have fewer layers of skin on the bottom of your feet than you do on most other parts of your body. That combined with the fact that the soles of the feet have no sebaceous glands makes it easier for oils to be absorbed there.

Plus, the warmed water can release the fragrance of the essential oils into the air around your chair. You get the added benefit of aromatherapy as your feet get a little vacation.

Words of Caution

Don't overdo it on the water temperature. You can experiment and go a little higher, but the idea here is to soothe your feet, not cook them.

When it comes to salt baths, Epsom salt is the usual go-to at a rate of one-half to one cup salt per one gallon of water. More is not better. Epsom salt is a magnesium sulfate compound. Some people experience a rash or hives when they use it at too high a dose.

Most essential oils that are used in the various following foot treatments should not present a problem when used at the recommended rate. However, if you have an allergic reaction to ragweed, for example, you might also react negatively to chamomile. Don't use an essential oil if you know you are allergic to that plant or flower.

Salt Baths

The easiest way to experience a salt-based footbath is simply to start with up to one cup of Epsom salt to one gallon of water. The magnesium helps reduce pain and swelling. The sulfate helps combat foot odors and bacteria.

Many commercial footbath preparations will include other salts in the mix. Dead Sea salt is especially popular due to its high mineral content. It is said to have ten times the mineral content of regular sea salt. Plus, it has a long history of safe and effective use to treat skin conditions, joint inflammation, and swelling.

Himalayan salt and Celtic sea salt have similar benefits. The only drawbacks relative to Epsom salt are availability and cost. If you have access to other types of specialty salts, it is perfectly fine to experiment with coming up with your own signature blend.

As for which essential oil to use, the sky is the limit. All essential oils are used at a rate of five to ten drops per gallon of water. You can dilute the essential oil in one ounce of a carrier oil like jojoba or grapeseed oil. This gives an added benefit of a moisturizer to your bath.

If all you are interested in is a relaxing soak, you can use any fragrance that appeals to you, from florals to spices. If you are looking for particular benefits, consider this:

- Lavender is the go-to for stress relief. Chamomile and vanilla essential oils will also help you achieve a sense of calm.

- Pine, juniper, and cedar are most often used for muscle aches. Rosemary, due in part to its "piney" fragrance, is good to use for this problem too.

- To cool hot and tired feet, try mints. Almost any of the mints will do, including peppermint and spearmint. Pennyroyal is one to avoid. It can be toxic even in small amounts. If you don't like the fragrance of mint, wintergreen is another essential oil that will reduce pain and swelling while leaving your feet feeling cool.

Bath salts can be blended for one-time doses to suit your mood. However, for convenience you can pre-blend your favorite oils and salt. Simply determine the number of cups in the bag of salt and add the correct number of drops of essential oil. Mix the ingredients in a large bowl to ensure you can stir the oils through the salt. Then, pour the mix into a large container that has a secure lid and store until needed.

Bath Bombs

Bath bombs are footbaths taken to the next level. Bath bomb recipes generally include baking soda and citric acid. Some people also use Epsom salt in their mix. The citric acid is what gives the bomb its fizz. The baking soda helps sooth inflammation and soften the skin.

The basic recipe is pretty simple. Use whatever essential oils suit your fancy. You will also need a large bowl to mix the ingredients in and molds to shape the bath bombs. The molds need to be at least one inch deep and large enough to accommodate roughly one half cup of packed mixture.

The classic shape is either a ball or a half ball. A small Pyrex glass bowl will work fine. You can find soap molds in most hobby shops and these will make excellent bath bomb molds.

You will need:
Paper to turn the bombs out on (butcher paper, wax paper, or foil)
1 cup baking soda
½ cup Epsom salt (optional)
½ cup citric acid
Dried flowers or herbs (optional)
10 drops essential oil
Uncolored witch hazel in a spray bottle

While making a small batch to start off with is a good idea for those who have never tried this before, this recipe can easily be doubled or tripled as needed.

Spread your paper out on the counter or tabletop where you are working. Measure all the dry ingredients in a large bowl. Ensure all the material is thoroughly mixed before adding the essential oil. If you would like to add some dried rose petals or minced mints or other herbs for effect, do so at this point.

Once the oil is added, spray the mixture with the witch hazel. Spraying allows you to control the amount of liquid that goes into the bombs. Start by completely dampening the top of the dry mixture. Then work quickly to blend the liquid into the dry batch. If you like the idea of adding color to the bath bombs, use any food dye you prefer. A few drops should suffice, but add as much as pleases you. Keep in mind that too much dye may stain your feet or your towels.

Add more witch hazel as needed. The consistency should be that of damp sand. Don't walk away at this stage! The mixture will "seize up" on short notice, and you'll be left with bath crumbles instead of bath bombs.

Once the consistency is right, press the blend into the mold very tightly until it won't hold any more. Tap the bomb out onto the paper and repeat the process until all of the mixture is used up. Leave the bombs to air dry for 24 hours. These can be stored in an airtight container until ready for use.

Herbal Footbaths

Herbal footbaths are just that—footbaths infused with herbs that have the same impact as essential oils. If the herbs you wish to use are flowers and leaves, make an infusion. In other words, bring 1 quart of water to a boil. Remove it from the heat source. Add 1 cup of dried or fresh herbs. Cover and let the herbs steep for 5–10 minutes. Strain and pour into 3 quarts of water that have been heated to roughly 104 degrees Fahrenheit.

Foot bones make up about a quarter of all the bones in the human body. The foot and ankle are made up of twenty-six bones, thirty-three joints, and over a hundred muscles, tendons, and ligaments.

If your herb mix is made from root, bark, and/or seeds, you will need a decoction. Heat 1 quart of water to a boil. Add the herbs and reduce the heat to low. Cover and allow to cook for 10–15 minutes. Strain and pour the mixture into 3 quarts of water that have been heated to roughly 104 degrees.

If your mixture includes both hard roots or bark and tender leaves or flowers, start as you would for a decoction. After the roots and bark have steeped for 10–15 minutes, remove the pot from the heat source and add the leaves and/or flowers. Let sit for another 5–10 minutes, then strain it into 3 quarts of hot water.

For ideas on which herbs to use for specific purposes (e.g., stress relief, cooling, etc.), refer to the list of suggestions in the section on salt baths. Truly, you can get very creative to come up with baths that are unique to your situation.

To get you started, consider this mixture. Bring 1 quart of water to a boil and add ⅓ cup of white willow bark. Turn the heat down, cover the pot, and let the bark cook for 10–15 minutes. Remove the pot from the heat source and add ⅓ cup each of eucalyptus and peppermint leaves. Cover the pot and let steep for 5–10 minutes. Strain the mixture and add it to 3 quarts of water that have been heated to roughly 104 degrees. Enjoy your soak.

After the Bath

How long you stay in the bath will be up to you. A general rule of thumb is about fifteen to twenty minutes or until the bathwater begins to cool, but stay as long as you like.

When the bath is done, pat your feet dry with a clean towel. Check for any issues like hang nails; damaged cuticles; dry, cracked skin; or bruising. Now would be a good time for a pedicure.

Before you complete your foot treatment, massage your feet with lotion. Let the lotion match the treatment. For example, a lotion scented with peppermint will keep your feet feeling cool. Floral-scented lotions engender a sense of luxury. Lotions with coconut oil or shea butter can address issues with cracked heels. Or you can just use your favorite hand lotion and enjoy the massaging action.

Finally, put your feet up and relax. Let that feeling rise all the way up to your tired shoulders and weary head. You've given yourself the gift of self-indulgence. Enjoy it until you are lulled off to sleep!

Resources

CDC. "Diabetes and Your Feet." Last modified May 7, 2021. https:// www.cdc.gov/diabetes/library/features/healthy-feet.html.

Epsom Salt Council. "Five Reasons to Soak Your Feet in Epsom Salts." Accessed September 20, 2021. https://www.epsomsaltcouncil .org/health/five-reasons-to-soak-feet-in-epsom-salt/.

Vagedes, Jan, Silja Kuderer, Eduard Helmert, Matthias Kohl, Florian Beissner, Henrik Szöke, Stefanie Joos, and Ursula Wolf. "Warm Footbaths with *Sinapis nigra* or *Zingiber officinale* Enhance Self-Reported Vitality in Healthy Adults More than Footbaths with Warm Water Only: A Randomized, Controlled Trial." *Evidence-Based Complementary and Alternative Medicine* 2021 (July 2021): 1–12. doi: 10.1155/2021/9981183.

WebMD Editorial Contributors. "Health Benefits of a Foot Soak." WebMD. Last modified June 22, 2021. https://www.webmd .com/pain-management/health-benefits-of-a-foot-soak.

The Six Medicinal Tastes in Ayurveda

❧ Janesh Vaidya ❧

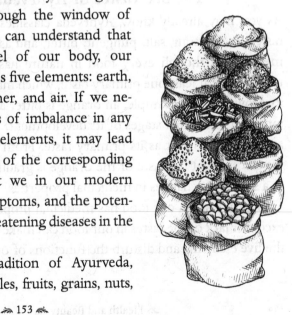

When it comes to food disciplines, Ayurveda, one of the most ancient health traditions in the world, gives specific recommendations according to the health condition of each person. By looking into our body through the window of Ayurveda, we can understand that the micro-level of our body, our cells, comprises five elements: earth, water, fire, ether, and air. If we neglect the signs of imbalance in any of these vital elements, it may lead to disfunction of the corresponding systems, what we in our modern times call symptoms, and the potential for life-threatening diseases in the long run.

In the tradition of Ayurveda, food—vegetables, fruits, grains, nuts, and legumes that we directly collect from the nature—is considered our primary medicine. Since Mother Nature constructed the particles of the food with the same five elements as our body cells, by the right intake of food, we can help correct many imbalances in our system.

Although we can't see these elements in our food with our bare eyes, we can sense them in each molecule of food by the taste we feel on our tongue. As the old saying in Ayurveda goes, our tongue is our eyes when it comes to the choice of our food. This means, if we keep our taste buds clean of food addictions, our tongue is our third eye, which can sense and lead our brain to take direction of our food choices. With conscious choices, we can reduce the use of the excess elements in our body by eliminating their presence in our diet and increase the use of necessary elements in our daily food that our body is lacking at present.

The Six Tastes of Ayurveda

As you may already know, Ayurveda classifies food into six tastes: sweet, sour, salt, pungent, bitter, and astringent. This means even though every food in nature has traces of all tastes, it has at least one primary taste, which may vary during its growth. As an example, an orange is bitter and then turns into sour in the first stages of its development. Then it ripens and becomes sweet as its primary taste. From this example, we can see that the taste of the orange is gradually changing as a sign of its changes in medicinal properties.

Every taste in our food has medicinal properties. But the excess or lack of the tastes in our food can make imbalances in the five elements and disturb the functions of our organs and systems. See the chart below, where the symbols minus (−), minus minus (− −), plus (+), and plus plus (++) indicate the influence of these tastes on the elements in our body.

Rasa (Taste)	Vata	Pitta	Kapha
Sweet	−	− −	+ +
Sour	−	+ +	+
Salt	−	+	+ +
Pungent (spicy)	+	+ +	−
Bitter	+	−	− −
Astringent	+ +	−	−

−	*decreases the force to a minimum degree*
− −	*decreases the force to a maximum degree*
+	*increases the force to a minimum degree*
++	*increases the force to a maximum degree*

With this simple knowledge about the natural properties of food, you can start your pharmacology from your kitchen and make medicine for you and your family rather than merely making food for survival. In the following sections I will discuss some of the most common health issues I noticed during my online consultations with clients around the world and the natural solutions I recommend based on the medicinal qualities of food, which I have gained from the tradition of my family.

Obesity

According to Ayurveda, obesity or excess body weight means that the levels of the earth-water elements in the body are higher than the normal condition. In the traditional practice of Ayurveda, a person's body weight is not taken as the primary parameter of health; instead, the weight at which they are comfortable to move freely and do a daily job while maintaining their flexibility, balance, and strength of physique is considered.

Are there any serious health issues if a person's body mass is higher than the optimum? Or, if I convert that question into Ayurveda terms, let me ask, if the earth-water elements in the body are high for a long period of time, is there a health risk?

According to Ayurveda, in a human body, the earth-water elements are forming the force of *kapha*, generating new cells, which are essential for the growth and maintenance of our body. But if these vital elements overrule the other elements (fire, air, and ether) in our system, there is a risk of accumulating *ama* (toxins) and excess *meda* (fat) in our *srotas* (channels) and thus generating obstructions in the circulatory system. These blockages in the blood vessels mainly create cardiovascular diseases, respiratory system disorders, sinusitis, high cholesterol and blood pressure levels, and related health problems. The accumulation of toxins attracts various kinds of pathogens to invade our internal systems and create diseases in our body.

With the help of the right diet and herbs, we can maintain our optimum body weight and healthy function of our circulatory system in all ages. To correct that imbalance in our body, we need to reduce the intake of the earth-water elements through our daily food consumption. And we should increase intake of food with higher properties of fire, air, and ether elements.

Now you may think, how do we know the properties of food? With the knowledge of Ayurveda and the help of our taste buds, we can sense the elements in each food. For instance, the food that tastes sweet and salty has a very high level of earth-water elements. So with obesity, we need to avoid and reduce the intake of salty foods, especially seafoods, and also sweet-property grains like rice and wheat, as well as wheat products like pasta, pizza, white bread, and so on.

To treat obesity, try eating food that tastes bitter, astringent, and pungent. The good news is most vegetables and spices come under this category. For example, the best options while designing a diet plan for obesity are vegetables like bitter melon, asparagus, aubergine, broccoli, brussels sprouts, and cauliflower; leaves like arugula; fruits like pomegranate and lingonberries; grains like quinoa, millet, oats, and barley; and legumes like adzuki beans, mung beans, and green and yellow peas.

In traditional Ayurveda, to reduce excess body weight, we use special herbs and plants that have the power to balance the earth-water elements in our body cells. Among them, the most common are the leaves of *punarnava* (*Boerhavia diffusa*) and *moringa* (*Moringa oleifera*), the roots of *chitrak* (*Plumbago zeylanica*), and the dry fruit of *bibhitaki* (*Terminalia bellirica*). If you are already familiar with Ayurveda medicines, you probably recognise bibhitaki as one of the three ingredients of *triphala churna* (three fruits powder).

When the kapha force is out of balance, the person can feel mentally sluggish and depressed. To the patients visiting my retreat in South India with this issue, we give *ashwagandha* (*Withania somnifera*) as an herbal intake together with other kapha-balancing treatments. The roots and the flame-colored fruit of ashwagandha are used in Ayurveda medicine to balance the level of cortisol in the body, normally associated with a high level of stress and depression.

Acidity

According to Ayurveda, our stomach is the cradle of our health, dominated by the fire-water elements in our body. Because of our modern lifestyle, many people in this world are suffering with stomach-related issues, and most are associated with hyperacidity, generated by our fast-food, fast-life culture.

Simply said, the stomach is the kitchen of our body, and it's essential that we have the right levels of fire-water elements in our system to maintain a perfect metabolism. If these elements are low in our system, we lose the appetite, which, as a result, causes poor digestion and malnutrition. But if the levels of fire-water elements get high in our system, they can aggravate the force of *pitta* and thus invite the symptoms and diseases related to that.

What are the main health issues caused by hyper fire-water elements in our body? During the three decades of my Ayurveda practice, I have noticed that many health issues are formed by the imbalance in these elements. In the early stage, physically, these imbalances can be shown as symptoms like headaches, eyepower variation, hair loss, a burning sensation in the esophagus, stomach pain, and skin problems such as eczema. If we neglect these signals from the body, these symptoms can develop to become tinnitus, migraines, drastic eyepower variation, psoriasis, ulcers, tumors, and cancers.

If you are aware of having any of the above symptoms or diseases, Ayurveda recommends avoiding food and drinks that have high properties of the fire-water elements and to adapt a diet with the healing properties of the earth, ether, and air elements. This change in your diet will not only balance the force of pitta but also heal the damages its excess caused in your system.

Here, again, we can use our taste buds to identify the food with healing properties to treat the pitta-aggravated symptoms and diseases in our body and mind. As a general rule in Ayurveda, if your fire-water elements are presently high in your system and showing corresponding symptoms, you need to avoid or reduce consumption of all foods and drinks that are pungent (spicy) and sour. And since salt has a certain level of pitta-aggravating properties, you should also be a little careful about salty food and eat it only in a moderate amount.

If you are suffering with any of the pitta-aggravated issues, you need to add food that tastes sweet, bitter, and astringent to your diet since these tastes have the property to heal the issues caused by the imbalance of the fire-water elements in your system. For example, leaves of neem (*Azadirachta indica*), *gulab* (*Rosa ×damascena*), and coriander (*Coriandrum sativum*) are commonly used in Ayurveda to treat pitta-aggravated symptoms. Apart from that, the dried ripe seeds of fennel (*Foeniculum vulgare*) and cardamom (*Elettaria cardamomum*) are also used to treat fire-water element imbalances in the body systems. By adding these leaves, roots, and seeds to your daily diet, you are actually increasing the intake of earth, air, and ether elements through your daily diet, which helps your internal system heal the damages caused by the hyperacidity in the body tissues.

When I mention the taste "sweet" in your food, please don't misunderstand: it is not just the sweets from a candy shop. Just as many vegetables have air-ether properties, and many fruits have sweet properties, which you can use as a natural medicine in Ayurveda to heal your pitta-aggravated symptoms. If you would like to know more about the list of foods and herbs with different properties (kapha-, pitta-, or vata-balancing food items), which have the natural power to cleanse and rejuvenate your system, before you go grocery shopping, you can visit my website at janeshvaidya.com /ayurveda/food and download a list of food and drinks available in stores in the United States.

Reproductive System Disorders

During my Ayurveda practice around the world, I have met many people suffering from the symptoms and diseases caused by the high levels of air-ether elements in their cells. In a balanced condition, these elements are playing a vital role in our body by supporting our internal systems to eliminate the toxins through the excretions. All the movements of the body, internal and external, are the result of the air-ether elements' corresponding force known as *vata*.

It's necessary to timely eliminate old cells and the waste particles of food and water from the body with the help of vata through sweat, urine, and feces, but if the air-ether elements are overruling our body cells at more than a certain level, the function of our entire system may eventually collapse. The aggravated force of vata may show in signs of poor digestion, like gas and bloating after eating, constipation and pain while excreting; hormonal imbalance (in women this could be menstrual disorders and difficulty getting pregnant); cold feet and palms; dryness of the skin and hair; pain in the lower back and joints; and mind-related issues like poor memory and focus.

If you are suffering with any of these issues, you can help correct them by changing your daily intake to a vata-balancing diet, which means a balanced diet favouring the tastes of sweet, sour, and salt, avoiding food that tastes astringent. Also, reduce the intake of foods that taste bitter and pungent, since they too have the property to trigger the force of vata, especially when it is already in a state of imbalance.

Do you know what herbs are used to treat vata-aggravated symptoms in traditional Ayurveda? In fact, vata imbalance in a system can be corrected in a very short time with the help of spices and herbs. Though most spices are good for reducing vata, some of them are more widely used in traditional Ayurveda to treat the illnesses caused by the air-ether elements in our body. Among them, poppy and mustard seeds are very common ingredients in Ayurveda recipes to balance these elements. Apart from that, cinnamon, asafoetida, cloves, and dry basil are used in Ayurveda kitchens when preparing food to treat the disorders caused by the force of vata.

Though garlic is used as a medicine to balance vata, from my personal experience, I can tell you that if you have insomnia or anxiety, it's better to avoid garlic in your food. Otherwise, it may worsen your sleeping issues and anxiousness. In that case, it is better that you add saffron to your food, especially in the evening, which will not only give you better sleep but also make your body warm and grounded. However, if you are pregnant, you need to consult your physician and an experienced Ayurveda practitioner to know the right amount of saffron to use in your daily food.

Adding one teaspoon of *haldi* (turmeric) in your food is a good habit, especially if you are constantly alerted by air and ether element symptoms. And if you have a habit of drinking tea, daily drink at least a cup of tea made with *brahmi* (*Bacopa monnieri*), which is considered a memory booster as well as a good source of antioxidants.

I have noticed that many people buy ashwagandha through online shops and take it without considering the present status of the elements in their body. Though ashwagandha is a stimulant widely used in Ayurveda to treat different alignments, especially for vata symptoms, if you are using it without knowing your PDE (presently dominating elements), there is always a risk to worsen the issues. To know your PDE, you can visit my website and do a self-test (janeshvaidya .com/ayurveda/test). It will take a few minutes, but with that wisdom you can add many more years of health into your life.

The Effects of the Six Tastes: Excess and Deficiency

As we have learned now, every taste has medicinal properties according to the dominating elements in it. And the right use of these tastes in our daily food can balance the elements in our body and keep a healthy system in all ages and seasons. But if any of these six tastes is used in excess or is deficient in our food, in the long run this may cause damage to our physical and mental systems.

Sweet: We have already learned that this taste increases the force of kapha and decreases pitta and vata. If we use this taste in excess, it may damage the pancreas and spleen and mentally make us feel too attached to worldly things and people. If this taste is deficient, it may cause malnutrition and lack of self-confidence.

Sour: This taste increases the force of pitta and kapha but reduces vata in our system. Overuse of sour may lead to liver and bile damages. Psychologically, ego and jealousy are associated with this taste. Sour has an important role in our digestive system, so a low level of sour food in our diet can cause gas formation in the stomach and, mentally, give us an inferiority complex.

Salt: Increases pitta and kapha but reduces vata. If we use too much salt in our daily food, it may damage the kidneys and adrenal glands and, in the mind, generate greed and dissatisfaction. The deficiency of salt can cause constipation and stiffness in the muscles and cause a negative attitude in the mind.

Pungent: Overuse of this taste heightens the level of pitta and vata. At the same time, pungent pacifies the force of kapha. As we know, too much spicy food can damage the functions of the stomach and esophagus. This taste is associated with anger and hate. A state where the spicy taste is lacking in our diet can slow down the digestion and also pull down our enthusiasm.

Bitter: The presence of this taste increases vata but decreases kapha and pitta. Though bitter taste has high levels of medicinal properties, extremely high amounts of this taste affect the heart function and damage the veins. Also, it can lead to sadness and depression in the long run. At the same time, if this taste is deficient in our diet, it can lead to the accumulation of toxins and additional fat in our system and may lead to obesity. In that state, the mind could be overruled by self-hatred and suicidal thoughts.

Astringent: The astringent taste increases vata but reduces the forces of pitta and kapha. Excess of this taste negatively affects the functions of the intestines and rectum. As a result, it shows in our behavior as nervousness and fear. In deficiency of this taste, the body tissues may grow inflamed and cause pain. Mentally, the lack of astringent taste leads to deep anxiety.

Foraging for Beauty

~ Charlie Rainbow Wolf ~

It's so easy to cruise the cosmetic counters or surf the online catalogs in search of something that's beautifying or age-defying, something that is a bit pampering and luxurious, something to help with the "feel-good factor," especially in recent months when life seems to have changed so much for so many people.

All these customs had a beginning, though: they were all born from traditions and practices handed down through previous generations. Our ancestors didn't have beauty shops; they had hedgerows and fields. They went foraging for their beauty—and so can you.

Basic Preparations

Before you start digging your dandelions or gathering your goldenrod, there are a few terms that should be understood. Not every item gathered will be suitable for every preparation. Understanding the fundamentals of kitchen cosmetics helps incur the success of homemade preparations. There are more processes than the ones I have listed; these are the ones I know work and the ones that are the easiest to do in the home kitchen—and at my age I tend to stick with what's simple yet effective!

Infusion

No matter how new you are to herbal preparations, chances are you have made an infusion. If you've ever made tea from tea leaves or a tea bag, you've made an infusion by "steeping" the tea. Infusions are usually steeped longer than teas to draw out more of the herbal properties into the water. It's also possible to use oil instead of water to infuse the herbs—one of the very first preparations I ever made was herbal infused oil for my auntie's arthritic hands. Simply warm the oil, suspend the herbs, and leave it to do its thing. (I left that first preparation in the airing cupboard, a small closet in the upstairs bedroom that housed the hot water heater, from one full moon to the next.)

Decoction

Some might say a decoction is just a really strong infusion, and this is a good way of looking at it. While to make an infusion the hot water or the warm oil is poured over the desired herbs, a decoction is made by simmering the herbs in the liquid until it is reduced by about half. This is perhaps a more effective method when using berries, bark, or seeds. Decoctions are more concentrated than infusions.

Tincture

Tinctures are similar to infusions or decoctions but alcohol or vinegar is used instead of water or oil. Tinctures are used with organic matter containing resins that are not water soluble. When vinegar is used, the finished item is usually referred to as a vinegar, rather than a tincture, such as "raspberry vinegar."

Essential Oil

This is often a sticky one, because what classifies as an essential oil is a slippery slope. The volatile oil of a plant is its essential oil; but what percentage is necessary for something to be a "pure" essential oil? At time of writing, there are no FDA regulations regarding essential oils. The FDA says itself that it looks at each situation case by case. It's been my experience that it is best to stick with oil infusions and not get into the distilling that accompanies making pure essential oils.

Cream

Creams are light and are made from approximately half water and half oil. They are hydrating and applied topically. It's an art to make a good cream, because getting the oil (or fat) and water to emulsify can be quite challenging.

Ointment

An ointment is softer than a balm or a salve. The recipe is very similar, but an ointment contains less beeswax (or carnauba wax, shea butter, or coconut oil if a vegan ointment is desired) and more oil. Coconut oil can also be substituted for the beeswax to make a softer preparation.

Balm

A balm's function is to sit on the top of the skin rather than to be absorbed by it. It contains no water (unlike cream), and is stiffer than an ointment. The preparation process is the same, and an ointment recipe can be turned into a balm simply by adding more beeswax.

Salve

A salve is the halfway point between an ointment and a balm—and perhaps my favorite of the three. I find it very easy to take herbal infused oil, add it to some beeswax (from the local bee-keeper), and decant it into squat two-ounce bottles. Boom, salve made!

Equipment Needed

Most of the tools needed when foraging for beauty and making the cosmetics are simply kitchen items. I do think it is a good idea to have different items from those used in food prep, though. Nothing bad is going to happen if you have to share; I'm just very aware of cross-contamination, especially if you plan on sharing your creations with others. Good hygiene is essential, even if you do have a separate set of tools.

Bucket

Not necessarily a kitchen item, but you'll want a bucket or large tub for collecting your wild harvest. This is one instance when I do use plastic over glass or wood; it is less likely to break and easy to clean. I've even used discarded gallon ice cream tubs in the past!

Snips

I have a small pair of pruning shears that I take with me. Heavy-duty scissors would work too. If you're adept with a knife, a pocket knife is also useful—anything to snip off what you're harvesting. The pruning shears work for me because I'm frequently gardening.

Measuring Jugs and More

Kitchen scales are extremely useful, particularly for weighing out things in grams when making small quantities. I have glass jugs in two sizes. These are for measuring the waters and oils and for the flora collected. Finally, I have a set of measuring spoons ranging from a quarter teaspoon all the way to one cup. I find I use the scales the most.

Glass Jars with Lids

Again, I have these in many sizes, from squat little two-ounce jars for packing finished salve in, all the way up to half-gallon canning jars with lids for steeping herbs and wildflowers. Pint and quart jars are good sizes for tea and other infusions like fire cider and vinegar preparations. I also recycle jam jars and other glass containers, taking care to wash and sterilize them before each use.

Cheesecloth

This is used for straining. I find it best to line a mesh sieve with the cloth and use them both simultaneously. This ensures that none of the debris from the plants used gets into your project.

Two Bits of Advice

Where, when, and how you forage for beauty will depend a lot on where you live! Here in south-central Illinois, there are lots of hedgerows with many useful wildflowers growing in them. I've also got quite an extensive wildflower and herb garden growing here at the Keep, our name for our little smallholding. Foraging is wonderful in that there are no hard and fast rules—but I will offer two points as a guideline.

First, ensure that you have permission to forage. The proverbial grass may indeed look greener on the other side of the fence, but obey the "no trespassing" signs if they're posted! I've found in the past that most people are agreeable to me foraging along their hedgerows provided I don't disturb their crops or their livestock.

Second, ensure that where you forage is safe. Do not collect plant material from roadsides. If you know there's toxic waste, effluence, or the overuse of pesticides or herbicides in the locality, it's probably wise to find a different—a better— place. Often just moving a short distance away will greatly improve the conditions.

Dandelion

I've put this first because, let's face it, nearly *everywhere* has dandelions! They seem to grow anywhere. I'm sure we baffle the neighbors, because we actually welcome them in the lawn. Their deep roots help to break up the areas of the yarden (yard + garden = yarden) where the soil is clayey and compacted. They're one of the first foods available to the bees and butterflies in the spring.

I remember hearing tales of dandelion roots being used as a coffee substitute during World War II, and a quick internet search will reveal that this is now something of a gourmet drink. Another popular drink is dandelion and burdock, made from the roots of these two plants. My dad put dandelion "greens" in his salads and soups.

Dandelion is useful in a home beauty routine. A vinegar infused with dandelion root makes a nourishing hair rinse. Use cider vinegar for dark or auburn hair and white vinegar for blond to get the best results.

✿ Dandelion Salve

Dandelion salve is easy to make and very soothing. Dandelions have a lot of antioxidants, including beta-carotene, which helps the skin maintain a healthy appearance. The salve is gentle yet effective when it comes to moisturizing and soothing minor irritations—including chapped lips and dry cuticles.

This salve is best made in the spring, when the dandelions are fresh and flush. Collect the flower heads and put them somewhere they can dry for a couple of days. An old window frame with a screen insert is a great idea, and a food dehydrator works too. This is to ensure that the moisture has gone from them, which will help the salve last longer.

Once they've dried, put them in a glass jar and cover them with oil. I like to use a combination of jojoba oil, sweet almond oil, and olive oil, but the actual choice is up to you. Coconut oil works just fine! The size of the jar will depend on how many dandelions have been collected and how much salve is being made. I use a 1-quart jar, half filling it with dandelion heads and then covering them with 1 pint of oil (the dandelions will take up too much room for a pint jar to be sufficient). From this I can get approximately 8 2-ounce pots of dandelion salve.

Leave the dandelion oil to infuse in a warm dark place for around 2 weeks. If you leave it longer than 1 month, it might spoil; the trick is to get the nutrients out of the dandelions without them starting to deteriorate. Once time has passed, strain out the dandelions from the oil through cheesecloth or muslin.

Beeswax is then added to the salve. You can also use carnauba wax, but less of this is needed as it is harder than beeswax. It's a matter of preference how much wax to add; the more the wax, the harder the salve. To 1 pint of oil I usually add ½ ounce in weight of wax to start; it's always easier to add more and make the salve harder than it is to try to soften it again. Store the salve in a cool, dark place. It has been my experience that it will keep well for over 1 year.

Rose (*Rosa rugosa*)

I have a love affair with wild roses. When I started working with foraging and wild harvesting, rose hip jelly was one of my first successes. Wild roses are so very useful, from their fragrant petals to their abundant hips—their fruit—to their protective thorns. We have just replaced a scraggly old hedge with *Rosa rugosa* here at the Keep.

Hedge roses, beach roses, and dog roses grow wild throughout the United States, Europe, and parts of Asia. If you're fortunate enough to live where there's access to them, great! If not, domesticated roses will work, but the fragrance might lack in potency, and the hips are likely to be insignificant.

Rosewater and glycerin composed the very first toner I ever used in my teenage beauty routine; my aunt let me try some of hers. Later I experimented with making my own. I'll admit the first attempt was sticky and not particularly useful, but that was because I used too much glycerin. Rosewater is useful for moisturizing while it is toning; rose petals are antimicrobial, confirms the *Journal of Environmental Science and*

Health. Do be aware, though, that rosewater has quite a short shelf life. Fortunately, it is easy to make: it can be made from dried petals, and—this bit is my favorite—it can be frozen. Make a big batch, freeze it in ice cube trays, and pop out what is needed when the time arrives!

Rosewater

To make rosewater, gather rose petals. The best petals are from freshly opened blooms, pesticide and herbicide free, and gathered early in the morning before the day gets too warm. I use a ratio of 1 part petals to 1½ parts water by volume. Distilled water is best; it eliminates any undesired chemicals creeping into the rosewater.

Wash the petals and add them to a pot of simmering water. It's important that the water is only just simmering; too hot and it will destroy the petals. Cook them until they have changed color, usually about 20 minutes. Let them cool in the water, then strain the liquid into sterile glass jars. That's it! Pop a lid on and it's finished. The water will store in the fridge for around 1 month.

Rosewater Toner

To make a glycerin and rosewater toner, add 1 part glycerin to 4–5 parts rosewater. This can be done at the time of bottling. The glycerin and rosewater are lovely and refreshing when applied using a mister bottle, but dabbing it on the skin using a cotton ball works just as well too. This is very soothing on minor irritations like sunburn or chafes, but avoid sensitive areas of the skin such as the nostrils or groin area.

A variation on this is to substitute the rose petals for cucumber. I often have more ripening cucumbers than I can use at once. I threw a couple into the blender, pureed them, and added them to some distilled water. I let them sit in the fridge overnight, strained them, and used them the same as rose water. The toner refreshed and soothed in the same way, and that fresh cucumber smell was divine!

Elder

Around where we live, elder grows everywhere. We have planted it in the yarden, but it is found in abundance along many hedgerows and stream banks and roadsides. I make jam with the flowers. We've been trying to make wine with the berries every year, but the birds always get to them before we do!

Elder is a wonderful old lady and needs to be respected. All parts of the plant are mildly toxic unless cooked. Elderberry vinegar is a soothing cold-weather cough remedy, but my preference for using elder is in the flowers. They can be added to honey for a nourishing face mask or steeped into a tea to use cold as a toner or hair rinse, and oil that has been infused with elderflowers is the foundation for a skin-softening salve.

✿ Skin-Softening Elderflower Salve

To make the salve, start by making the elderflower oil. This recipe is very similar to the dandelion salve (see page 171), swapping the elderflowers for the dandelion heads. I find that a 1-quart jug of elderflowers will compact into the jar nicely once I've removed the flowers from the stem, still leaving room for the oil. I use half jojoba oil and half sweet almond oil for this.

Strain the oil and add the wax, as per the dandelion recipe. I use less wax with elderflowers than I do with dandelions, for

I want this to be a softer balm. I have contemplated whipping this with shea butter to make a body butter but haven't tried it yet (if you do, please drop me a line and let me know how it goes!).

Goldenrod

Goldenrod grows profusely around here and is considered a weed. I don't pull it unless I have to. I have it growing next to the house along with ironweed—another "weed," as if the name wasn't a clue—and they look divine with their mustard yellow and deep purple flowers. As well as being aesthetically pleasing, goldenrod is also valuable in home herbal and kitchen cosmetic preparations.

⁂ *Goldenrod Lotion Bar*

Most of my kitchen cosmetics start out as an oil infusion, and the goldenrod lotion bar is no exception. I collect the young flowers in the morning, preferably on an overcast day. For this infusion, I use approximately 12 ounces in volume of coconut oil, warming it gently before pouring it over the goldenrod flowers, and keep it in a warm, dark place while they infuse. Coconut oil is solid at room temperature and shouldn't solidify before it has absorbed the properties of the goldenrod.

Once the oil has been strained into a glass jug, I warm the coconut oil until it is fluid and add around 8 ounces in weight of cocoa butter (this is also fairly solid at room temperature) and 1 ounce of beeswax; this is more than goes into the salve, but the finished product is a bar, so it needs to be more set.

When all three solids are warm and fluid (but not hot; this destroys their healing properties), pour the liquid lotion into a mold. I use silicone molds but anything will work; I've lined jam jar lids with parchment paper before today! Allow to cool thoroughly before removing from the molds—at least half an hour, but I leave mine overnight just to be sure. Made this way, the lotion bars are solid at room temperatures (unless you live in the tropics) and do not need to be refrigerated. With the cocoa butter and the coconut oil, they smell absolutely amazing too!

Beauty in Your Backyard

I feel I've barely scratched the surface on what beauty products can be made from wild-harvested plant matter. The best advice I can offer next is to leave you with a bibliography for further reading, so you can dive down the rabbit hole and explore your own environment. Look at what grows wild, what is abundant in the area. Find its botanical name and then research its benefits and uses. Here, we have many things that are seeding themselves in the yarden, from black-eyed Susans to purslane, from poke to pigweed, and I know that it all has some kind of use, some kind of benefit, even if it seems a nuisance to me at first.

One thing the last three years have taught me is that many lessons I need to learn are waiting for me in my own backyard, or not far from my own doorstep. Nature knows what is needed, and when I work in harmony with what is local, rather than fighting against it or looking further afield, that is where I find my most profound answers. I wish you the same experience and the same awakening—and the same enjoyment—as you delve deeper into what can be created in your own kitchen, by your own hand.

Resources

Center for Food Safety and Applied Nutrition. "Aromatherapy." US Food and Drug Administration. Last modified August 24, 2020. https://www.fda.gov/cosmetics/cosmetic-products/aromatherapy.

Easley, Thomas, and Steven H. Horne. *The Modern Herbal Dispensatory: A Medicine-Making Guide.* Berkeley, CA: North Atlantic Books, 2016. Pages 25–26.

Zhang, Wenluo, Fawzia H. Abdel-Rahman, and Mahmoud A. Saleh. "Natural Resistance of Rose Petals to Microbial Attack." *Journal of Environmental Science and Health, Part B* 46, no. 5 (May 24, 2011): 381–93. https://doi.org/10.1080/03601234.2011.572502.

Further Reading

Landreau, Gabrielle. *101 Homemade Beauty Products Recipes: Make Your Own Body Butters, Body Scrubs, Lotions, Shampoos, Masks, and Bath Recipes.* Self-published, 2015.

Little, Kitty. *Kitty Little's Book of Herbal Beauty.* London: Jill Norman, 1980.

Maury, Militza. *Natural Homemade Skin Care: 60 Cleansers, Toners, Moisturizers and More Made from Whole Food Ingredients.* Salem, MA: Page Street, 2020.

Newcomb, Lawrence. *Newcomb's Wildflower Guide.* Illustrated by Gordon Morrison. New York: Little, Brown and Company, 1989.

Thayer, Samuel. *The Forager's Harvest: A Guide to Identifying, Harvesting, and Preparing Edible Wild Plants.* Bruce, WI: Forager's Harvest Press, 2006.

DIY
and
Crafts

The Craft of Nettle Cordage

✑ Rachael Witt ✑

The leaves are turning into colors of red, orange, and yellow with a golden hue. Jays are alarming in the hazelnut trees as squirrels drop hulls of black walnuts and caps of acorns from overhead. The plant seeds are ripening before the mold sets in from the autumn rains. In between seed stalks and branches, spiders are weaving webs to capture the season's spread of insects. The harvest time of year is at its climax, reminding me of the offerings of plants in their various stages of their life cycles. Roots, stalks, leaves, flowers, fruits, and seeds—the abundance is clear. On the fall equinox, my harvesting includes plants for food, medicine, and seasonal crafts.

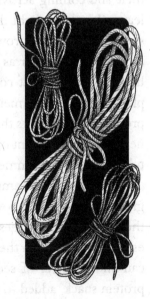

Stinging nettle calls to me at this time of year. There's nothing like bowing down to the tall, grooved stalks to capture the fullness of this plant's growth. Lowering myself to the base of the nettle, being mindful of its protective stinging hairs, I extend my gratitude to its gifts by harvesting the stalk for fiber. Carefully dodging the spider webs, I make my way to another tall stinging nettle plant to cut, strip, and add to a bundle of processed stalks. The spiderwebs are most everywhere, inspiring me to prepare for the seasonal craft of weaving. It's here that I would like to share with you the technique of working with stinging nettle in the fiber art of cordage.

The Uses of Nettle

Stinging nettle has been increasingly gaining attention. It's not surprising because this herb is also one of my affection. There's nothing like walking on a trail as the winter snows melt and coming across the first sprouts of unfurling nettle leaves. It's this delight that reminds me of the fresh tastes of spring and the new growth to appear.

Nettle is popular as a springtime edible and a nourishing herbal ally. We most commonly harvest and work with this plant until early summer. Once the plant puts on its flowers, it produces constituents that make it less digestible. This is when nettle becomes a plant of awareness—one that teaches us how to move in its environment without being stung.

Starting late summer and into autumn, stinging nettle grows tall. It shoots above the blackberry brambles and meets the height of small trees. In some places it makes a nettle forest of its own. From the underside of each opposite leaf, one can find a cluster of seeds. The seeds can be collected for a protein snack, added to a tincture for adrenal support, or left to grow starts for the next year. When the seeds are ripened for harvest, this also indicates that the stalks are ready to be processed into a wild fiber.

It takes about two stalks of processed nettle fiber to make a necklace or hat band.

The Craft of Cordage

Cordage is also known as cord, thread, or rope. According to Heidi Bohan's book, *The People of Cascadia*, cordage is "fiber twisted into strands ranging in size from thread to thick rope." This is an ancient craft. It is a craft of natural material that has many utilitarian purposes. Traditionally, people used cordage to make fishing nets, bowstrings, basket straps, clothing, and jewelry and to lash structures together. Cordage can be made using many different types of plant fibers, animal sinews and hair, or synthetic materials. In the Pacific Northwest, the Coastal Salish people used nettle as one of many natural materials to make cordage. When I learned this, my admiration for nettle grew even more. This plant is edible, medicinal, and utilitarian. Like so many herbs, the art of natural cordage comes from the story of the harvest, the processing and preparation of the fiber, and the making of the cord itself.

The Harvest

Walking among the stinging nettle forests, I see the plants' long stalks leaning down toward me. Some of these stalks can be eight feet tall! These are what I look for when harvesting nettle for cordage fiber. To harvest the stalks, I recommend wearing a pair of gardening gloves. Follow the stalk to the base and use a harvesting knife to cut right above the ground. In this way, the rhizomes of the plant will stay intact. With one hand holding the tip, use the other hand to wrap around the stalk, making a fist form. Slide this hand toward the base of the plant, crushing the stinging hairs and stripping the opposite leaves and seed clusters. Disperse the leaves and seeds around the area of harvest to encourage new growth in the coming years. Place the stripped stalk in a noticeable area and continue harvesting a few more stalks to process into fiber. To further ensure the return of the nettle patch, follow the one-in-ten harvesting rule: for every ten stalks, harvest one.

Processing and Preparing the Fiber

1. Dry

Once I have a handful or so of nettle stalks, I bundle them together and tie them with a string, rubber band, twist tie, or nettle stalk itself. I hang the bundle upside down or lay it on a screen, ensuring that there's good air flow to dry the fibers out. Drying the stalks out makes it easier to process the fiber. It also allows for a tighter wrap when making cordage (wet fibers will eventually dry out and shrink, leaving the cord loose). Depending on the temperature and drying place, the stalks can take 1–5 days to completely dry. This is most noticeable when the stalks turn a light green/yellow/brown color and they feel dry to the touch.

2. Flatten

Once the stalks are dry, it is time to peel off the outer fibers from the inner pith of the stalk.

To do this, I like to take a rock or heavy stick and lightly hit the stalk on a flat surface to flatten it. Another way of doing this is by stepping on the stalk. Either way, make sure that the stalk is flattened on two surfaces. Next, pick up the stalk and use your thumb to slide open one of the seams. I pretend that I am opening a book, so that the inner pitch is now exposed and lying flat.

3. Peel Away the Inner Pith

Using one hand, hold the stalk about 1 inch from the wide end, having the inner pith of the stalk facing you. With your other hand, break the top end of the stalk away from yourself. The lighter-colored inner pith should have a crack where it broke, whereas the outer darker-colored fibers will bend in this process. Peel the broken inner pith away from the outer fibers by pulling upward. There should now be 1 inch or so of fiber lying over the forefinger of the hand holding the stalk. Take these fibers and peel them from the inner pith by pulling them away from you and downward while supporting the fibers with the forefinger of the hand holding the stalk. The goal is to peel the outer fibers away from the inner pith, stop, and then break off 1–2 inches of the inner pith before peeling the fibers away more. Ideally, the outer fibers stay together as the inner pith is broken off.

To further remove any small pieces of inner pith from the outer fiber, place the fiber in between your two hands and rub them together. The friction of your hands will also buff the fibers. This is a slow process that allows for soft fibers that can be twisted together. Ensure that all the inner pith is removed and set the fiber aside before starting on your next stalk.

Making the Cordage

The method to making cordage is called reverse wrap. This technique can be done with multiple fiber strands—and it's always best to start with a simple two-strand or "two-ply" method. In this way, the two strands will be twisted and then wrapped around each other in the opposite direction. Follow these steps (adapted from Bart and Robin Blankenship's method in *Earth Knack*):

1. Wet the fiber strands with water.
2. Take the strand of fibers from one stalk (or combine two for thicker cord) and find the center.
3. Hold the strand by placing your right thumb and forefinger about ½ inch away from the center and your left thumb and forefinger about ½ inch away on the opposite side from the center.
4. With your right thumb and forefinger, twist the fibers away from you, while twisting the fibers in your left thumb and forefinger toward you. This should create tension and a small loop will twist in the center.
5. Pinch this center loop with your left thumb and finger, keeping the two strands separated. One strand will be on the right side and the other strand will be on the left side.
6. Continue pinching this loop and use your right forefinger and thumb to twist the right strand away from you.
7. When it is tightly twisted, bring this right strand toward you and lay it over the left strand, switching the right and left strands. The "left" strand is now on the "right" side.
8. Take this new right-side strand, twist it away from you until it tightens, and then bring it toward you and lay it over the new left-side strand. Again, switch left and right strands.

9. As you twist and alternate strands, the cord will begin to form. Keep the two strands separated and secure by pinching your left forefinger and thumb along the center point; this also creates tension away from the strands as you twist.

10. Alternate twisted strands and repeat this process until the cord is finished.

11. To extend the length of the cord, splicing is required. To do this, add a new fiber over 3–4 inches of the old strand. Roll them together in the process of twisting the right strand away from you, then bring the spliced strand toward you and over the left strand. Switching the left strand to the right side, add in new fiber to this new right side strand.

12. When the cord is complete, tie both strands together with an overhand knot to keep the ends from unraveling.

The strength of the nettle cordage depends on the number of strands used to reverse wrap.

Uses of Cordage

Cordage is most commonly known as an art of bushcraft (the use and practice of skills in order to survive and thrive in a natural environment). It is a fundamental craft that binds tools used to harvest food and tie structures together for shelter and fire craft. It is also a beautiful way to turn nettle fiber into cord, thread, or rope. I use nettle cordage to embellish baskets or add to hat bands. I often use it to hold containers, water bottles or keys. Nettle cordage can be used as jewelry, strung with natural beads for a necklace or tied around your wrist as a bracelet. I'll even use it to wrap mugwort, sage, and yarrow into smudge bundles for ceremony. Each twist of the fiber and wrap around the bundle is made with intention. The art of making nettle cordage is an honoring of the plant for its gifts not only as food and medicine, but also its utilitarian uses as well. And perhaps that is reason enough to make and use nettle cordage.

References

Blankenship, Bart, and Robin Blankenship. *Earth Knack: Stone Age Skills for the 21st Century.* Salt Lake City, UT: Gibbs Smith, 2008.

Bohan, Heidi. *The People of Cascadia: Pacific Northwest Native American History.* Seattle, WA: 4Culture, 2009.

De la Forêt, Rosalee, and Emily Han. *Wild Remedies: How to Forage Healing Foods and Craft Your Own Herbal Medicine.* Carlsbad, CA: Hay House, 2020.

Makah Museum. Accessed March 16, 2022. https://makahmuseum .com/.

Apples All Season Long: Easy Grafting Techniques

⚞ Monica Crosson ⚟

In the eastern corner of Skagit Valley in Washington state, rivers cut through mountains, creating narrow valleys that trap the clouds and keep those who inhabit the area under a perpetually weeping sky. Here our trees as well as our homes are coated with moss, our feet are always damp, and our gardens are home to more slugs than earthworms or ladybugs, but we wouldn't have it any other way. The people who inhabit this area are a strange lot—lost souls, dreamers, and artists who are drawn to the songs that sweep through the low-hanging mist of old-growth forests—and I'm proud to call these people my friends.

One such friend is a violin maker and musician whose sweet offerings have been known to bring the burliest of souls to tears. He is also a skilled saber fighter and has trained me, and many others, how to wield a sword through our local HEMA organization. If that isn't enough, he is also our valley's own Johnny Appleseed, freely sharing his knowledge of growing and grafting fruit trees with anyone who would like to learn. A couple of years back, I told him about the difficulties we were experiencing in my own small orchard. My older trees, it seemed, had lost their vigor. I was worried I was going to have to take them out completely and start over with saplings.

"Before you do that," he said. "Let me take a look."

He came to my house on a gray and drizzly January morning and inspected my old trees. We talked about shape and the varieties of apples that would grow best in my micro-region. Two weeks later, he returned with a small chainsaw and clippers, and we got to work. The trimming was hard for me to do, as I had always been much more delicate with my topwork (too delicate, it turns out). After the work was complete, my trees were ready for phase two of their extreme makeover.

With the arrival of spring, my friend returned with scion wood and grafting tape in hand, and he, my son Elijah, and I got to work. He taught us an easy method known as "bark grafting," and by the time we were finished, three of my five apple trees had four varieties each that would allow for continuous harvesting throughout mid-summer to fall.

After the process was complete, my first thought was, why hadn't I done this before? It really was that easy. Of course, the fact that I was grafting older trees increased the chances for failure, but of the dozens of grafts we did that day, only one failed (and it was one that I had done). And the best part is, by grafting, I was able to ensure that I had apple varieties that not only would thrive in my micro-region but also suited our culinary wants and needs throughout the harvest season.

Grafting Basics

When we walk through the forest in winter, the soft rattle of branches moving in the breeze can be a soothing sound. We look up and see a lacework of branches intricately woven (so it seems) against a pale sky and smile at the wonder of it all. But once in a while, trees' branches get locked together in such a way that the continuous pressure wears away the outer bark, revealing the cambium layer, and over time the two branches fuse together. This is a spontaneous graft that happens in nature.

The propagational art of grafting is a technique that has been practiced for thousands of years. It is believed to have originated in the colder northeastern regions of Asia, and though there is no recorded history of the invention of the technique, historians believe that the method was most likely based on those observations of spontaneous grafting that could be seen in the forest.

In modern times, grafting is used by horticulturists for many reasons, the most important being to produce plant varieties that are identical to the original source. Other reasons include better disease and pest resistance, optimizing cross-pollination, and the ability to withstand specific climate conditions. It's commonplace for many nurseries to use the technique, and chances are that you have a plant in your garden that started from a graft. Many ornamental plantings, such as Japanese maples, flowering cherries, and camellias, are created from grafts. Apple trees are always grafted because they are hybrids and not true to seed.

Grafting basically describes any number of techniques in which a stem with buds (called a scion) is inserted into a rootstock. The scion becomes the desired plant, and the rootstock becomes the trunk. When choosing plants to graft, remember rootstocks and scions from the same species are always compatible (apple stem to apple rootstock) and rootstocks and scions from the same genus are also usually compatible (plum stem to peach rootstock). The further up the taxonomic triangle you go, the less compatible the plants become.

There is a myriad of grafting techniques in use today. Here are some of the most common:

Side-Veneer Graft: A popular technique for grafting conifers and usually done on potted rootstock.

Cleft Graft: An extremely simple grafting procedure for top work in both fruiting and flowering trees.

Whip and Tongue Graft: A strong-holding graft used most often on woody ornamentals.

Bridge Graft: Used to bridge damaged or diseased plants and provides a way to allow nutrients and water to move across damaged area.

Saddle Graft: Any easy method used on dormant stock that is no more than an inch in diameter.

Bark Graft: Primarily used on fruiting and flowering trees and can be applied on rootstock of a large diameter.

The Bark Graft Method

The bark graft method is what we used on my older apple trees as a quick-and-easy alternative to replanting my small orchard. This form of grafting can only be done in early spring just as buds are beginning to open. What I like about this technique is that it is easy for the beginner and has a relatively high success rate.

You will need:

Good, sharp pocketknife (You can invest in a grafting or budding knife, but it's not necessary.)

Small hammer

Brad nails

Grafting tape

Grafting compound

You will also need scion wood. These cuttings should be from the previous year's growth, 6–10 inches long, straight, about ¼ inch thick with 3–4 buds. They can be purchased from most orchards after trimming during the dormant season or ordered online. Another way to acquire scion wood is by asking friends who grow apples to give you a few stems after they have trimmed their trees in late winter. Some areas also offer scion wood exchanges.

Step 1

During the late winter when trees are still dormant, you need to cut back the tree(s) you are grafting within 1–2 feet of where you wish to place your grafts. If you ordered your scion wood online, it should arrive in early spring. When picking scion wood for your apple tree grafts, keep in mind your wants and needs. Consider taste, season and keeping qualities, disease resistance, and varietal suitability for your micro-region. If you acquired scion wood from a friend or local orchard, make sure the cuttings are pest and disease free. Wrap the stems in a damp paper towel, peat, or sawdust; place them in a sealed plastic bag; label them; and store them in the refrigerator until you're ready to graft.

Step 2

During early spring, just as the buds begin to open and the sap starts flowing, it's time to graft your tree(s). Cut another 2 inches of wood to expose a live end from areas you wish to place your grafts.

Step 3

Using a sharp pocketknife, make two vertical cuts (1½ inches in length and the width of your scion wood) approximately every 2–4 inches around the circumference of the surface of where you are placing your grafts. Only slice through the bark to reveal the green cambium layer. The cambium layer is responsible for the new growth and bark, so it's important that your scion wood matches up to it.

Step 4

Again using your sharp pocketknife, make an outside diagonal cut, leaving an exposed area of approximately 1½ inches along the end of your scion wood. Repeat this cutting technique on the opposite side. The end of your scion wood should resemble a chisel.

Step 5

Carefully insert the scion wood under the bark up to the scion wood's cut surface. Continue this process around the circumference of the stock.

Step 6

Use the small hammer to gently tap a single brad through the bark and scion wood. Wrap the area around the grafted stock with grafting tape. Use grafting compound to seal the end of the tape, then use it to seal the exposed stock and the tops of the scion wood.

Remember to check your grafted apple tree's seals weekly and repair when necessary. If it's not raining, provide your grafted tree with at least 5 gallons of water per week. Prune any new growth on the rootstock (not the scion wood), as it draws energy from the new grafts. You can remove the grafting tape after you see new growth (1–3 months). Depending on the care and the variety of apple, it can take 2–3 years before you see fruit. But that's okay. It will be worth the wait.

Apple Varieties

Graft several of these apple varieties to a rootstock for an extended harvest from July through October:

July to August Harvest

Gravenstein (July to August): This wonderful dessert apple yields crops of medium fruit with red-over-green skin. Great for baking and sauces or just for snacking.

William's Pride (Late July to August): A quality, disease-resistant apple, this medium-size red fruit has a sweet, rich flavor.

Lodi (Mid-August): Great for cider, pies, and applesauce, this yellow transparent apple is large and tasty.

Zestar (Mid-August): This cold-hardy, early-season apple is sweet and tangy and keeps in proper refrigeration for up to two months.

Ginger Gold (August): Juicy and delicious, this apple features a yellow-green skin with a golden glow. It has a crisp crunch and mildly tart flavor.

Jersey Mac (Late August): With bright red-green skin, this
apple has a strawberry-like flavor and bright white flesh.
Perfect for eating or baking.

Paula Red (August to September): Paula Red boasts a red color
with light yellow striping and has a sweet, tart flavor.
Great for baking.

September Harvest

McIntosh: Medium-size fruit with red and green skin and a
bright apple aroma. Wonderful apple for fresh-eating,
sauces, and cider.

Honeycrisp: Outstanding fresh-eating qualities make this variety an American favorite. The fruit is aromatic and sweet
with a juicy bite.

Golden Delicious: Large golden apples with outstanding flavor. An instant favorite for baking, salads, or snacking.

October Harvest

Keepsake: Small, irregularly shaped, and red in color, these
are crisp and juicy. They keep well for up to six months.

Northern Spy: Northern Spy is an old-fashioned standby that
retains its popularity. It is a typical winter apple variety
that keeps in a cold store well into spring.

Blushing Gold: Firm and tangy, this apple is able to last
through the winter if you keep it chilled. With a pleasant
pink blush over yellow, its full, rich flavor improves after
time. It's great for dehydrating.

Granny Smith: The classic baking apple is firm and juicy. It's
one of the best to bake and cook with and a favorite for
dipping with peanut butter, and it won't brown quickly,
making it ideal for salads, fruit platters, freezing, and more.

Pink Lady: This tart-sweet apple has a beautiful, bright white flesh that is slow to brown, making it extremely versatile, and can be used for baking, snacking, salads, or sauce.

Evercrisp: A cross between Honeycrisp and Fuji, Evercrisp is a very firm apple with a very sweet flavor. Keeps exceptionally well.

Fuji: The juicy, ultra-sweet bite makes this large apple a best seller. Its very long shelf life makes it a perfect storage apple.

Seasonal Doll and Creature Crafts

⇾ Autumn Damiana ⇽

I know what you are thinking...this must be a "girly" craft article. Only women and girls like dolls, right? Not so! Dolls have a long history as toys for children of all genders, but they also exist as entertainment for adults, like puppets and marionettes. Additionally, dolls can be found in religious ceremonies, fertility spells, and even as funerary figures throughout the ages.

But what exactly is a "doll"? Modern dolls are typically used as playthings, like the stereotypical "babies" that girls use to play house and mimic parenting, or the figure dolls that older girls and boys use during dramatic play. But then there are some "dolls" that cross the line into other domains,

like mannequins, stuffed animals, action figure toys, figurines, and collectibles. My geeky husband who collects Star Wars toys will tell you in no uncertain terms that his action figures are *not* dolls. But really, a doll can be any material object that assumes a familiar form, like a human, animal, or mythical being.

This article explores the myriad forms that a doll can take and gives instructions on how you can make these for yourself. In reality, most of these projects are not "dolls," in the humanoid sense. Many are animals or other creatures, but they are created for the same purpose as any modern doll, which is to bring a pleasant experience of childlike enjoyment and symbolic meaning to the creator, owner, and collector.

To make these crafts as easy as possible, most of them utilize a hot glue gun because the glue will adhere to most surfaces and will become permanent as soon as it cools. If you don't have a hot glue gun, you can get one at any craft store, usually for under ten dollars plus the cost of the hot glue sticks. Have fun with these seasonal crafts that you can make throughout the year for holidays, gifts, or just something fun to do with your children or friends. Happy crafting!

Spring

≫ No-Sew Bunny Buddy

This is a really cute craft you can make for spring holiday baskets or gifts. The best part is that the bunny can be heated in the microwave to make a warm, snuggly bedtime friend for a fussy or sleepless child. Fluffy socks work best, but any sock will do.

You will need:

- 1-pound bag of rice
- A few handfuls of fresh, strong-smelling flower petals (lavender, rose, gardenia, jasmine, etc.)
- Essential oils (optional)
- 1 crew or tube sock
- Scissors
- Twine or string
- Permanent marker
- ⅛–¼-inch wide ribbon (optional)
- Embroidery thread and needle (optional)

In a bowl, mix together the bag of rice and all the flower petals. The petals should be fresh because they will dry out naturally in the rice and give it scent. You can also stir in a few drops of essential oil if you want.

Stuff the sock with 1 cup or so of the rice and flower mixture. Use twine to tie the sock shut just above the rice. Make the knots tight so no rice falls out. The unfilled portion of the sock will become the ears.

Mentally divide the filled portion of the sock into thirds. Use the twine to separate and tie off the top third to make the head.

Flatten the sock above the head and cut off all but 4–5 inches. Then cut through both pieces in a V shape to make ears. Trim each ear further to get the shape you want.

Draw dots on the face for eyes and an X for the nose and mouth. You can embroider these features instead if you like, and/or tie the ribbon into a bow around the bunny's neck.

Take care to not use metallic ribbon or ribbon with wire inside, as this cannot go in the microwave.

Warm up your bunny in the microwave for 30 seconds and check that it is not too hot before giving it to a child.

❧ Sprout Pet Turtle

Here is a fun way to add a little greenery to a room with minimal effort. These sprouts are extremely easy to grow and care for, and when they start to fade, you can pull them out and begin the project again!

You will need:
- 1 tablespoon chia seeds
- Bowl
- Wooden spoon
- 7-inch cork trivet
- Hot glue gun and glue
- 4 wine corks
- Craft saw
- Sandpaper (optional)
- Green acrylic paint and paintbrush brush (optional)
- Googly eyes
- Spray bottle with water

Put the chia seeds in a bowl and cover them with water. Let them soak overnight. They will develop a jelly-like consistency that will help them stick.

Lay the wooden spoon faceup across the middle of the cork trivet so that the spoon part sticks a little more than halfway over the edge. Hot glue the spoon in place on the trivet. This is the bottom of the turtle.

Around the bottom where you have glued the spoon, glue the four wine corks standing up so that they make legs.

Cut the handle of the spoon short so that about 2 inches stick out from the edge of the trivet. This is the turtle's tail. Sand the tail end if you want it to be smooth.

You can now paint the turtle legs, head, and the tail with green acrylic paint. When dry, flip the turtle over and glue googly eyes on the turtle's head.

When the seeds are ready, spray water on the turtle's back until the cork is damp. Pour out the excess water from the chia mixture, stir it, and spread it evenly with no clumps over the cork trivet.

Spritz your turtle with water multiple times throughout the day so it doesn't dry out. You will soon see chia sprouts.

Summer

✎ Edible Potato Head

It can be challenging sometimes to get your child to eat their vegetables. As a teacher, I have found that one way to motivate them is to get them involved in some part of the eating process, like growing their own vegetables or having them pick out the vegetables at the store or farmer's market. Then you can try this fun cooking trick at home.

You will need:
    Large thin-skinned potato (yellow or red)
    Cooking knife
    Decorative vegetables (see instructions)

Toothpicks

Scissors

Basting brush

Olive oil

Baking sheet

Prick the potato all over with a knife tip. Then heat the potato in the microwave. This will cook the inside, and then you can bake the skin in the oven later. Most microwaves have a potato setting, but you can also put it in for 4 minutes on one side and then flip it over for another 4 minutes. If you can push a fork easily into the potato, it is done. Otherwise, repeat for 1 minute on each side.

Let the potato cool enough to be handled, and then get creative! Use small circles of zucchini for eyes, slivers of bell pepper for mouths and eyebrows, cherry tomatoes for a nose, cauliflower or broccoli florets for hair, carrot or celery sticks for arms, mushroom buttons for feet, and so on. Use canned items like olives, "baby corn," or water chestnuts in a similar manner. Attach your decorative vegetables to the potato with toothpicks cut in half.

Roast the potato head in the oven. Brush the potato head and all the vegetables with olive oil and bake on a baking sheet in a 425°F oven for about 30 minutes to crisp the potato skin. This will shrivel all the vegetables, so tell your children what to expect or let them check the progress periodically through the oven door glass.

Plate your potato head and eat! Remove all the toothpicks before serving it to younger children. Pair it with butter, sour cream, and chopped herbs like dill, parsley, green onions, and chives.

⚘ Simple Corn Husk Doll

These dolls are plentiful at almost every late summer fair and harvest festival. They have their origins in Native American practices but today are enjoyed by all cultures to celebrate the gathering of the corn. This is a shortcut to make this doll that works well for children or anyone who has tried this craft and has found it difficult. Use green corn husks that you shuck yourself, or get these from a friend or at a summer barbecue.

You will need:

> 7 green corn husks
>
> Natural-colored jute or hemp string
>
> 1 chenille stem (pipe cleaner)
>
> Fabric or fleece scraps
>
> Scissors or pinking shears
>
> Hot glue gun and glue

Lay 6 of the corn husks together. Tie them together with string ½ inch from the top.

Invert the corn husks and fold them down, so that the tied part is inside. Grasp them together under this part and tie it with string. This will make a rounded "head."

Make arms by rolling up the chenille stem in the remaining husk. Separate the husks beneath the head so that you have three in front, and three in back. Push the rolled-up husk up the middle to just under the head, at right angles to the rest of the body. It will look like a cross. Tie the husks together just underneath the arms to hold them in place.

If you want a doll with a dress, you are finished. To make a doll with pants, once again divide the 6 husks, this time with

3 on the left and 3 on the right to make legs. Tie these with string at the ankles and at the knees.

Bend the arms into whatever shape you like, and put the doll away someplace safe and airy to dry out completely until it turns beige and feels stiff and crinkly to the touch.

Cut clothing for the doll out of fabric using scissors or pinking shears and secure them with hot glue. You can cut a square or rectangle with a hole in the middle for the doll's head to make a poncho or sleeveless tunic, and use strips of fabric for scarves, hats, bonnets, belts, and the like.

Fall

⋙ Spooky Apple Head Mummy

Apple head dolls are an old-time craft that has been in use in the Appalachia region of the United States for centuries, but here I present it with an autumn twist. This can be a tricky craft project because you don't know what you are going to get—every head turns out different and unique. But that's half the fun!

You will need:
Several large firm apples (Granny Smith are perfect)
Paring knife
Dried corn cob (make sure to cut away all the corn kernels and let it dry out)
1 tablespoon salt
2 ounces lemon juice
2 ounces water
Bamboo or metal skewer
Toothpicks

Hot glue gun and glue

White fabric (you can use an old t-shirt—the more tat-
tered, the better)

Plan on making a few heads so that at least one will yield
the expected result. First, peel the apple with a paring knife
(you can also use a vegetable peeler). Discard the peel.

Use the paring knife to cut features onto your apple. This
is an intuitive process—there is no right or wrong way to do
it. Start by carving circles into the apple where the eye sockets
would be. Then cut a line straight down from the inside of one
socket and then the other, about ¾ inch. This is the bridge of
the nose. Remove some of the apple on either side to accen-
tuate the bridge. Cut around the end of the nose and remove
some of the apple there also. Last, under the nose, cut a wide
slit across to make a mouth. Define your features further if you
like. Make further cuts around the eyes and mouth for wrinkles.

Mix the salt with the lemon juice in a small dish until it
dissolves and then add 2 ounces of water. Place the apple head
in the mix, turning every 30 minutes until all sides are equally
saturated.

Repeat the carving and saturating steps with the remaining apples.

Drying the heads is a matter of climate. If you live somewhere that is humid, begin the drying process by putting the
apples in the oven on the lowest temperature for at least 6 or
more hours. Use an oven-safe glass dish. Then you can hang
them by their stems or on skewers somewhere airy and dry
where they will not be disturbed and can age for the next few
days or weeks. If you live in an arid or desert environment,
you can skip the oven drying.

You will know when the apple heads are done because they will shrink quite a bit and feel dry and leathery, with the appearance of wrinkled old people.

Now you will make your mummy. Choose an apple head and stick it to the corn cob with a combination of toothpicks and hot glue.

Cut or tear the white fabric into long strips. Wrap them around the corn cob and the apple head, taking care to leave most facial features exposed. Use the hot glue gun to anchor each fabric strip in place.

☙ Autumn Turkey Gourd Centerpiece

This is a really fun way to serve appetizers at your next fall gathering. You can use different sized gourds or even a pumpkin (which counts as a gourd), depending on how many guests you expect.

You will need:

 8–12-inch terra-cotta saucer

 Hot glue gun and glue

 Flat thumbtacks

 Medium to large decorative gourd or pumpkin

 Whole cloves

 Paring knife

 1 orange

 Red vegetable/fruit (bell pepper, tomato, strawberry, etc.)

 Toothpicks

 Scissors

 Bamboo skewers

Seasonal decorations (acorns, pinecones, colorful leaves, flowers, whole nuts, cinnamon sticks, star anise pods, etc.)

Appetizers on skewers

First, you need to secure the gourd so it will stand upright. Use a hot glue gun to glue flat thumbtacks (flat side down) into the center of the terra-cotta saucer; use 3 to 7 depending on the size and weight of the gourd. Make sure to use lots of glue to hold the thumbtacks in place. Next, impale the gourd on the thumbtacks in the position you want it to stay in.

Make the turkey face. On the front of the gourd, use whole cloves for eyes, and cut a triangular beak from orange peel. Make a wattle for the turkey with bell pepper, tomato, strawberry, or another red food. Secure them with toothpicks, and cut off the ends. You can also use whole cloves studded into the front of the gourd to give the turkey the appearance of breast feathers.

Peel the rest of the orange in ribbons and arrange the peels inside the terra-cotta saucer around the gourd. Add other seasonal decorations that smell or look nice.

Assemble the skewered appetizers. Keep them simple. Try layering basil, cherry tomatoes, and mini mozzarella balls for a caprese salad. Or alternate mint leaves, strawberries, and chunks of feta if you are experiencing warmer weather. Once you have the skewers ready, jab them into the back of the gourd in a semicircle to make the turkey's tail. Use scissors to cut off the ends of the skewers if necessary.

If you are having trouble pressing the cloves or skewers into the gourd, use the tip of the paring knife to make small but deep X-shaped cuts and then press the cloves or skewers into the middle of the X.

Winter

⚘ Holiday Stick Gnomes

I love how these figures stand up and peek out of a garden or a potted plant, depending on the size. They also make whimsical gifts and are fun to create with a group of people for a winter holiday craft project.

You can use just about any kind of wood to make these gnomes. I've had good luck with pine, redwood, and fruitless mulberry.

You will need:

Wood branches (sticks)

Wood-carving knife or whittling knife

Acrylic paint (skin tone of choice, red, and white)

Paintbrush

Black permanent marker

Clear acrylic sealer (optional)

Carve one end of the stick into a long point with the knife. Then cut off one side of the point at a 45-degree angle to make that side flat. This flat area is the gnome face that you will paint.

Paint the entire face with your choice of complexion, any skin tone from light to dark. Then paint the top half of the point red, like a hat. Finally, paint a white beard around the bottom of the face and up the sides. Use a permanent marker to draw two dots for eyes.

Brush clear acrylic sealer over the face if you want to make the design water resistant and last longer.

ᕼ Scented Pinecone Fairy

Because this is another kid-friendly craft, it can be a fun activity for your children to make as a present or to simply decorate a wreath or tree with. Experiment with the components of the aromatic mixture and make several different batches to see what you like best.

You will need:
  Sturdy pinecone
  1-inch round unfinished wood bead
  Yarn
  Hot glue gun and glue
  Aromatic holiday spice mixture (see below)
  Mortar and pestle
  White glue
  Cotton swabs
  Bowl
  Felt scraps
  Markers or colored pencils

Stand the pinecone upright and glue the wood bead on the top to make a head, with the hole running vertically.

Take a piece of yarn 4 inches or longer and make a loop, tying it together with a knot at the bottom. Secure the knot inside the bead head with hot glue.

Prepare the aromatic mixture using holiday spices. Choose from balsam, cedar, pine, sage, bay, cinnamon, ginger, allspice, clove, nutmeg, juniper berries, star anise, orange peel, grated apple, and other favorite spices. Use only whole herbs and spices and make sure everything is dried. Break up larger components, like cinnamon sticks and pine needles, by hand. Then put all your ingredients in the mortar and pestle and crush them together until you have a grainy (not powdery) blend.

Use the cotton swabs to dab globs of white glue inside the scales of the pinecone near the center.

Hold the pinecone over a bowl and sprinkle it with your aromatic mixture, turning the pinecone until all the gluey spots are covered. Shake off the excess, and repeat if necessary.

Decorate your fairy. Glue on yarn strands for hair and felt wings, and draw a face on the wood bead with the markers or pencils. You can also use the felt to make a hat, scarf, or even mittens for the fairy.

Plant
Profiles

Plant Profiles

This section features spotlights on individual herbs, highlighting their cultivation, history, and culinary, crafting, and medicinal uses. Refer to the key below for each plant's sun and water needs, listed in a helpful at-a-glance table.

Key to Plant Needs	
Sun	
Shade	—
Partial shade	☀
Partial sun	☀ ☀
Full sun	☀ ☀ ☀
Water	
Water sparingly	◗
	◗ ◗
Water frequently	◗ ◗ ◗

USDA Hardiness Zones

The United States is organized into zones according to the average lowest annual winter temperature, indicating a threshold for cold tolerance in the area. This USDA Plant Hardiness Zone Map uses the latest available data. For best results, plant herbs that can withstand the climate of their hardiness zone(s) and bring less hardy plants indoors during colder weather. Seek additional resources for high summer temperatures, as these can vary within zones.

It is helpful to keep track of temperatures and frost dates in your neighborhood or check with a local gardening center or university extension for the most up-to-date record. Climate change and local topography will also affect your growing space, so compensate accordingly.

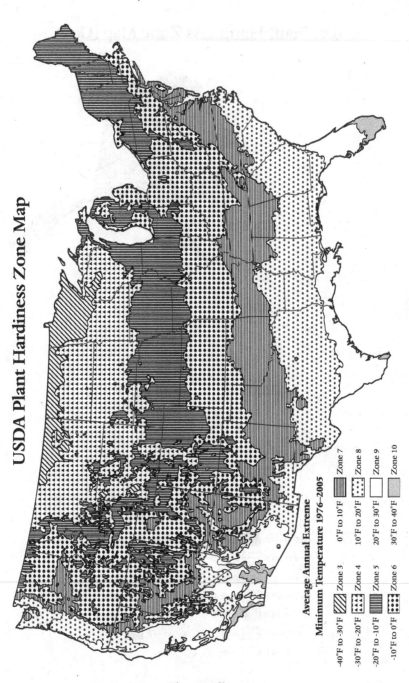

USDA Plant Hardiness Zone Map

Average Annual Extreme Minimum Temperature 1976–2005

- Zone 3: -40°F to -30°F
- Zone 4: -30°F to -20°F
- Zone 5: -20°F to -10°F
- Zone 6: -10°F to 0°F
- Zone 7: 0°F to 10°F
- Zone 8: 10°F to 20°F
- Zone 9: 20°F to 30°F
- Zone 10: 30°F to 40°F

USDA Plant Hardiness Zone Map (Cont.)

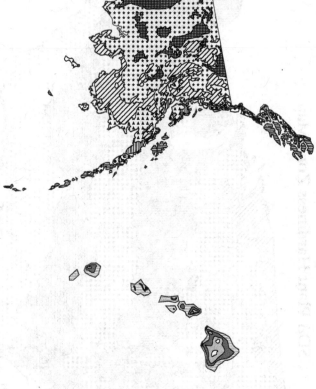

Average Annual Extreme
Minimum Temperature 1976–2005

-60°F to -50°F	Zone 1	10°F to 20°F	Zone 8
-50°F to -40°F	Zone 2	20°F to 30°F	Zone 9
-40°F to -30°F	Zone 3	30°F to 40°F	Zone 10
-30°F to -20°F	Zone 4	40°F to 50°F	Zone 11
-20°F to -10°F	Zone 5	50°F to 60°F	Zone 12
-10°F to 0°F	Zone 6	60°F to 70°F	Zone 13
0°F to 10°F	Zone 7		

Mustard

✎ Anne Sala ✎

Mustard is a tiny seed, but its impact on the world's well-being and taste buds is huge. As one of the first domesticated plants, its piquant qualities have found its way into countless foods. The seeds are used in sausage, in jars of pickles, as a cooking spice, and as a traditional condiment for meals across China, Europe, and North America. When I make homemade macaroni and cheese, mustard powder is one of the ingredients! For something so commonplace, it would be easy to take it for granted, but when a person wants mustard, they want it in a specific way and no other way will do. Try it—think about the taste of mustard. Are you thinking of the flavors of a

Mustard	
Species	*Brassica* spp.
Zone	6–11
Needs	☀☀☀ 💧💧
Soil pH	6–7
Size	2–6 ft., out and up

backyard barbecue? A hearty Sunday dinner? A sandwich from a delicatessen?

Mustard is a member of the Brassicaceae plant family, along with broccoli, kale, turnip, and horseradish. There are over forty different varieties of mustard plants with three different seed colors. Black mustard seeds (*Brassica nigra*), called *sarason* or *marathi*, come from India and were heavily traded throughout the ancient world. Today, a lot of the seeds are crushed to produce a pungent oil. It is used in cooking as well as medicinally for various skin, hair, and joint ailments. References to the medicinal use of mustard can be found on Sumerian cuneiform tablets from 2000 BCE.

Mustard with brown seeds (*Brassica juncea*) originated in the Himalayas, and when the Romans built their empire, they brought brown mustard to use as a vegetable and the black mustard seeds as a spice.

Yellow or white seeds (*Sinapis alba*, syn. *Brassica hirta*) originated in the Mediterranean, and Egyptian pharaohs were buried with pots full of it to use in the afterlife. The Greek word for mustard is *sinapi*, which means "that which troubles the eye."

Mustard plants are an edible wonder and notably nutritious. Their roots, stalks, leaves, flowers, and seeds can all be eaten. The greens are a good source of vitamins C, K, and A; calcium; and copper, making it a welcome early spring vegetable to forage after a long winter. The seeds contain fiber, manganese, magnesium, and selenium as well as some unique components.

When mustard seeds are ground up, the powder is odorless, but when mixed with a liquid, an enzyme called myrosinase goes through a chemical reaction that produces an oil called allylsenevol. This is responsible for mustard's pungent, tongue-tingling, sinus-burning, eye-watering qualities.

While tending the mustard in my garden, I occasionally bit into a seed to see what would happen. When the seeds were young and green, I could detect the familiar taste of mustard, but none of the spiciness. Later in the season, as the pods started to dry, the seeds I chewed started out innocently with no chemical reaction. But as soon as I opened my mouth to say, "I think there's something wrong with my mustard seeds," my breath activated the mustard oils and my tongue started to burn. Success!

In India the saying "to see mustard flowers" means to faint or be dazed from a shock or strong smell.

Mustard is a hardy annual. It flourishes in nearly any type of soil and is drought tolerant. It can even withstand frosty early autumn temperatures, but it can bolt if it gets too hot. Mustard is one of only a few spices to be cultivated in temperate parts of the world, such as Nepal, Canada, and Hungary. Depending on the variety, the plant can grow from two feet to over six feet tall. The leaves are deeply lobed and range in size from two inches to over a foot long. In mid-summer, mustard will send up four-petaled yellow flowers that make the shape of a cross. This is why members of the mustard family are also called cruciferous, which means "cross bearing."

Along with being a profitable food crop for human consumption, mustard makes a beneficial green fertilizer. Farmers will plant it in the fields after the cash crop is harvested. Then, before the mustard sets its seeds, the whole plant will be mowed or plowed into the soil to decompose, replenishing depleted nutrients.

Growing and Harvesting
Mustard in Your Home Garden

Growing mustard at home is easy. I began researching this article while still in the dark days of the COVID-19 pandemic when I wasn't visiting stores in person. I went to my spice cupboard and pulled out a bottle of yellow Andante mustard seeds distributed by Burlap & Barrel. I sprinkled about fifty seeds in my garden and lightly covered them with soil. Within three days, I had sprouts.

If sowed in the spring, mustard will grow steadily. Young leaves can be used in salads. A little later on, when the plant is about eight to twelve inches tall, one can harvest stems or the whole plant to use in stir-fries, kimchis, and pickles. At this point in the summer, there is still time to plant another round of mustard seeds. After the flowers fade, long seed pods will grow.

Once the pods get knobby and start to brown, they can be harvested for the seeds. Fine hairs on yellow seed pods dry out and can irritate your skin, so be careful. (Apparently, brown mustard pods are not hairy and might be a better choice for home gardens.) Cut the branches off and place them in a paper bag. Store the bag in a well-ventilated area for at least a month or until the pods burst open with only slight pressure from your fingers.

The mustard plants I grew did not want to give up the ghost after I cut the seed-bearing branches. They sent up another round of flowers, and I was able to harvest even more seeds after the first hard frost of fall.

To collect the seeds, I suggest planning your setup carefully. They are small, and when the pods are popped open, the seeds can zing every which way. Harvest them on a breezy, sunny day.

You will need:

  1 large tea towel

  1 punched metal colander that has holes slightly bigger than the mustard seeds

  2 plates

  1 shallow teaspoon or flat-bottomed measuring spoon

  1 funnel that has a mouth that fits in the jar

  1 clean, dry jar with lid

Lay out the tea towel on your work surface to collect wayward seeds.

Situate the colander on top of one of the plates and set aside.

Place the second plate and teaspoon on the tea towel in front of you. Bring up the first branch of seed pods and pop them open on the plate. If the pods don't want to open easily, just put the whole pod onto the plate and gently crush it with the back of the spoon.

When you have a fair amount of seeds and broken pod pieces on your plate, tip them into the colander. Gently stir the contents to help the seeds pass through the holes.

Once you have processed all your pods in this manner, or once the plate is getting full, use the breeze to help winnow the seeds. Scoop up seeds and the chaff that fell through the colander and let them trickle back onto the plate. The breeze will blow the hairs and pod pieces away. Do this several times to remove as much chaff as possible (there might always be a little).

Set the funnel's mouth into the jar and carefully pour the seeds into the jar. Don't forget to add any seeds that fell onto the cloth!

Therapeutic Uses for Mustard

In Ayurvedic medical research, mustard seeds are noted for their ability to heat up the body: physically, by warming the skin when applied topically, and internally when ingested, by causing a spicy sensation in the mouth and nasal passages. Mustard is used to help treat inflammation, fungal infections, and respiratory illnesses. Smearing a mustard "plaster" on the skin was a common treatment for colds and pneumonia. Today, this treatment isn't used as much because it can cause irritation. A less intense approach that also has a long therapeutic history is taking a mustard bath.

⁂ Mustard Bath

You can add any essential oils that you wish, such as lavender if you are trying to promote sleep. This recipe has peppermint and eucalyptus, which will help relieve congestion when fighting a cold. I recommend purchasing the mustard powder in bulk from a spice company, like Penzeys Spices, rather than buying bottles at the grocery store. The first time you use this concoction, I suggest first making a foot soak so you can see how your skin reacts. Your body will still reap plenty of benefits.

You will need:

1½ cups Epsom salt

1 cup mustard powder

1 cup baking soda

10–15 drops peppermint essential oil

10–15 drops eucalyptus essential oil

Combine all ingredients in a bowl and stir with a large fork or whisk, breaking up any lumps. This recipe makes enough for 3–6 baths. Store the contents in an airtight container.

When ready to use, fill the bathtub or footbath with water as hot as you like. Add 1 cup of the mixture to the bathtub or ¼ cup to the footbath. Soak for 20 minutes. You will probably notice your body sweating. Afterward, shower your whole body, or rinse your feet, in tepid water. Dry off, rubbing your skin vigorously, then bundle up and allow your body to continue to sweat. Take this opportunity to rehydrate with cool (not cold) water or warm (not hot) herbal tea.

Making Prepared Mustard

The French are responsible for the plant's modern name because of their practice of combining mustard seeds with unfermented grape juice. This was called *mustum ardens* in Latin, or "burning must." To this day, the region of Dijon is known for its delicately flavored prepared mustard, considered some of the best in the world.

When I look at a shelf full of mustards at the grocery store, I am amazed at the variety. Smooth, lumpy, brown, yellow . . .

green? Surely there's a secret trick to making this stuff—there's no way someone could make it at home. It turns out there is no trick. It can be as simple as mixing a spoonful of mustard powder with a sprinkling of flour and water to serve with a Sunday roast. The English have done this for over two centuries with Colman's Mustard, a nasal-clearing condiment that looks like the innocent yellow mustard used in the States. I spent a semester abroad in Norwich, England, the home town of Colman's, and I learned about it the hard way when I asked for mustard on my hamburger at a fast-food joint!

⪺ Herbes de Provence Mustard

This mustard starts out hot but will mellow with age. A few days after it is made, you can adjust the seasonings if necessary. This recipe makes about ¾ cup.

You will need:

⅓ cup yellow mustard seeds

1½ teaspoons yellow mustard powder

½ cup water

1 tablespoon wheat flour

¼ cup rice vinegar or champagne

1 tablespoon white sugar

2 teaspoons dried herbes de Provence mix, lightly crushed

1 teaspoon salt

Grind the mustard seeds with a mortar and pestle or an electric spice mill until just barely broken up.

Dump the seeds and mustard powder into a wide ceramic or glass bowl and mix with water. Cover the bowl with a cloth and leave on the counter for 3 to 24 hours. Stir occasionally. It will thicken significantly.

After the mustard has rested, whisk in the flour until smooth. Then whisk in the vinegar, sugar, herbs, and salt.

To smooth out the texture, you may run some or all of the mustard through a food processor or blender, but this is optional.

Store the mustard in a clean, dry jar with a lid. If kept on the counter, it will continue to mellow. Refrigeration will allow it to retain some of its heat.

In Germany, brides will sew mustard seeds into the hem of their wedding dresses in order to ensure they rule the house.

✎ Garlicky Mustard Greens

I initially thought I would scour my books and the internet for the most innovative use of mustard greens I could find, but I decided against that after sautéing some last night and realizing that this was still my favorite way to eat them. Basically, the recipe is the same as one would use for spinach, but the end result is a bit more sharp. This recipe serves 4 and is perfect paired with teriyaki chicken and steamed rice.

You will need:

    1 pound mustard greens, rinsed thoroughly
    2 tablespoons toasted sesame oil
    2 garlic cloves, chopped

2 tablespoons soy sauce

1 teaspoon rice wine vinegar, or to taste

Salt and pepper to taste

Trim the cut edge of the mustard leaf stems, then chop the stems into bite-size pieces. Set aside.

Chop the mustard leaves into bite-size pieces and set aside, separate from the stems.

Set up a pot with water and a steamer insert and bring to a boil. Drop in the stems and allow them to cook for 1 minute. Add the chopped greens to the stems and cook for an additional 2 minutes.

Meanwhile, heat the sesame oil in a wide pan over medium heat and sauté the garlic until fragrant, about 30 seconds.

Using tongs, add the mustard greens to the garlic in the pan. Pour in the soy sauce and vinegar. Stir to coat. Add salt and pepper to taste. Serve immediately.

ᨓ Mustard Soup

This is the "ultimate" mustard recipe. *Mosterdsoep* is an iconic soup from the Groningen region of the Netherlands. It reminds me of the creamy and tart flavor of beer cheese soup, and the traditional garnish for it is bacon. This recipe serves 4.

You will need:

3½ tablespoons unsalted butter

1 small onion or shallot, chopped finely

½ cup all-purpose flour

4 cups chicken or vegetable broth

2 tablespoons prepared mustard, either smooth or grainy (or a combination of both)

½ teaspoon yellow or brown mustard seeds

½ cup heavy cream

Salt and pepper to taste

4–6 slices bacon, cooked crisp and crumbled

Melt the butter in a large saucepan or dutch oven over medium heat. Add the onion or shallot and sauté until translucent, 3–5 minutes.

Sprinkle the flour over the onion and stir to form a paste, or roux. Keep stirring for about 1 minute, then add the mustard and stir to incorporate.

While still stirring, pour in the vegetable broth. Allow the mix to come to a boil.

Add the mustard seeds and cream. Season with salt and pepper and allow the soup to just barely simmer for about 10 minutes.

Ladle the soup into bowls and garnish with bacon. Serve immediately.

I find it comforting to think of all the generations of humanity that have enjoyed mustard's unique properties. Whether in the kitchen, bathroom, or apothecary, this tiny but mighty seed has left its fiery mark on the world, binding us together.

Resources

Benjamin, Sarah Kate, and Summer Singletary. *The Kosmic Kitchen Cookbook: Everyday Herbalism and Recipes for Radical Wellness*. Boulder, CO: Roost Books, 2020.

Encyclopaedia Britannica Online. S.v. "mustard." Accessed October 15, 2021. https://www.britannica.com/plant/mustard.

Engelbrecht, Karin. "Groninger Mustard Soup." The Spruce Eats. Last modifed March 24, 2021. https://www.thespruceeats.com /groninger-mustard-soup-recipe-1129049.

McGrane, Kelli. "Mustard Greens: Nutrition Facts and Health Benefits." Healthline. March 25, 2020. https://www.healthline.com /nutrition/mustard-greens-nutrition.

Mills, David G. "Mustard: Growing Guide for the White & Black Mustard." Wild Foods Home Garden. Accessed October 30, 2021. https://wildfoodshomegarden.com/Mustard.html.

Stewart, Martha. *The Martha Stewart Cookbook*. New York: Clarkson Potter, 1995.

Witty, Helen. *The Good Stuff Cookbook*. New York: Workman Publishing, 1997.

Bay

≈ Kathy Keeler ≈

I love finding that a plant I thought I knew only as a name is in fact a familiar plant. That was the case for bay. I knew bay leaves were a dried spice sold in grocery stores. I knew Olympic victors wore crowns of laurel leaves. Then one day I learned they are the same plant!

Bay and laurel are alternate common names for a tree from Greece, Italy, and surrounding areas. The scientific name is *Laurus nobilis*, in the plant family named after it, the laurel family, Lauraceae. *Laurus* was the traditional Roman name for the tree, and the species epithet *nobilis* means, as you would expect, renowned, notable, excellent, famous. Sometimes, the common names are combined as

Bay	
Species	*Laurus nobilis*
Zone	8–10
Needs	☀☀☀ 💧💧💧
Soil pH	4.5–8
Size	up to a 40' tree, 30' across

bay laurel, or it is called sweet bay. You also see it referred to as Roman, Grecian, or Turkish laurel. In both English and Italian, other plants have similar names; the bayberry of New England (*Myrica*), used for candles, is not related, and *lauro* in Italian is the cherry laurel or English laurel (*Prunus laurocerasus*), a shrub with leaves similar in shape to bay but which are poisonous.

Growing Bay

Bay trees are native around the Mediterranean, so once established, they grow well in California, which has a similar climate. They have been planted successfully across the southern United States but grow poorly in wet soil and can survive only a light frost. Although slow-growing, bay trees can reach more than thirty feet tall and spread twenty feet. They tolerate pruning, even radical pruning, and so can be grown as hedges or shrubs. The familiar oval leaves of the herb are a glossy dark green on the tree and have a lovely aroma. In the spring, bays produce clusters of pale yellow-green flowers that develop into black berries. They are evergreen, keeping their attractive leaves all winter.

Bay trees grow nicely indoors as well. I grew one in a pot for about twenty years. It started a few inches high, gradually growing to be almost four feet high. Actually, it did nothing for several years, not dying but not adding any leaves. I don't know if it had been shocked by its time in plant stores or if the conditions I gave it were unsatisfactory. Eventually, though, it started growing, to the point I struggled to keep it a manageable size. I never saw it flower, but it donated many leaves to my kitchen. I gave the tree away ten years ago, deciding that, in its big pot, it had gotten too large for my house. It is still alive, growing well on a closed porch. It was an undemanding, attractive houseplant and a dependable source of bay leaves.

The California bay tree, *Umbellularia californica*, is a relative. When I lived in California, before the little bay tree mentioned earlier came into my life, I used California bay leaves when a recipe called for bay leaves. They are in the same plant family, Lauraceae. The substitution worked okay for adding "bay-ness" to the food, but I like Grecian bay better; the flavor of California bay is not as mellow.

Bay in History and Myth

The Greeks were using bay more than 3,000 years ago. The tree was so important that it had a myth that explained its origin. In the myth, the god Apollo was stricken with love for the river nymph Daphne. She refused him and fled. Apollo pursued her, entreating. Not wanting him to catch her, Daphne begged her father, the river god Peneus, to put her beyond Apollo's reach. Peneus turned Daphne into a bay tree. Apollo, sincerely grieving, vowed to honor her forever. From then on he wore a wreath of laurel leaves. He declared the tree sacred and gave it the gift of eternal youth; the bay tree is evergreen. Despite his philandering, Apollo was a beloved god; anything he honored was thought very worthy. The myth is told several ways since various regions claim to be the place where it happened; for example, the river god might be Ladon in Arkadia or Amyklas of Sparta. In Greek and subsequent European cultures, not only was bay widely used in food and healing, but laurel wreaths crowned victors in contests from athletics to poetry.

The tradition of recognizing success with a wreath of bay leaves persists today. We don't often wear real wreaths on our heads, but metaphorically we do; the baccalaureate recognizes the success of a bachelor's degree; the poet laureate is an honored poet; the Nobel laureate won the Nobel prize; and, conversely, "resting on your laurels" is to do nothing after a dramatic success.

The magic of bay extended farther. People for hundreds of years believed bay protected them from lightning and forest fires. Whenever thunder was heard, the Roman Emperor Tiberius anxiously set a laurel wreath on his head. Bay defended from the supernatural as well; standing under a bay tree, you were safe from witches and the devil.

Bay in the Apothecary

Bay has been used medicinally for millennia. Dioscorides, in his *De materia medica* in 64 CE, recommended bay as an astringent, to treat wasp and bee stings, and for pain in the ears. By the time of Nicholas Culpeper (1616–54), bay was a veritable cure-all. Culpeper, who wrote one the earliest medical books aimed at a popular audience, recommended it for gall stones, obstructions of liver and spleen, against the poisons of all venomous creatures, pestilence, and infectious diseases, to aid in childbirth, for colds, coughs, eye or lung injuries, shortness of breath, and headaches. Bay also expelled wind, provoked urine, killed intestinal worms, and made menstruation more regular. That's only about half of what he used bay for, but you get the idea. To see the whole list of what bay was believed to do, find Culpeper's *The Complete Herbal*, which is available both online and in bookstores.

Today people treat conditions including diabetes, cancer, pain, and stomach problems with bay, but no strong scientific evidence supports those applications. Bay leaves, wood, and berries contain a diverse array of chemicals: carbohydrates, alkaloids, steroids, flavonoids, tannins, triterpenoids, phenols, citric acid, and the essential oil. The essential oil you see for sale is made by steam distilling the leaves and consists of eugenol (clove oil), estragole (major component of tarragon), eucalyptol, myrcene (a common terpene with a pleasant odor), and trace amounts of other compounds. Weak infusions of bay leaves or berries stimulate appetite. The oils in bay can irritate the skin, and some people are allergic. These problematic compounds are stronger in the fruits (berries) and in the essential oil than in the leaves.

Extracts and oils from bay will poison snails and other molluscs, kill microbes, and repel insects. Historically, people knew that and laid bay leaves in clothes chests to discourage pests. These properties likely help bay salves and oils treat skin or ear problems from bacteria or fungi. Bay also has strong antioxidant properties, promising for future drugs.

The insect-repellent characteristics are still employed in natural gardening. One way would be to plant the trees around the garden. Alternately, spread bay leaves on the soil to discourage insects.

On the branch, bay leaves are stiff and dark. They make a nice accent in fresh or dried flower arrangements.

Commercially, bay is an ingredient in many food products but is also included in liqueurs and cosmetics such as colognes and aftershaves.

↬ Bay Potpourri

Fragrant and stable, bay leaves are wonderful in potpourri. Put dried bay leaves in a bowl, alone or with other fragrant leaves, to add floral scents to a room.

You will need:

- 6–8 roughly crushed cinnamon sticks
- 6–8 roughly crushed nutmeg seeds
- Dried eucalyptus leaves (about ½ cup)
- 15–20 bay leaves roughly broken
- 2–3 tablespoons orris root powder (from roots of European iris, a scent enhancer and preservative)
- ½–1 cup dried flowers or flower petals for color

Mix all the ingredients together. Makes 3–4 cups.

Cooking with Bay

Most of us know bay as a spice. My mother's spaghetti sauce required it, "but never more than two leaves—they're strong." Cooking with bay leaves goes back to at least ancient Greece; recipes using bay leaves appeared in one of the first European cookbooks printed, Platina's *On Right Pleasure and Good Health*, from Italy about 1470. Bay's strong, resinous taste is not something you want to bite into or savor on your tongue, but it adds wonderful depth and complexity to foods. It is a secret ingredient, hardly noticed, but taking the dish out of the ordinary. You find it in recipes for soups, stews, stuffing, sausages, meat and seafood dishes, vegetable dishes like bean and pea soup, and an array of sauces. A bay leaf is added to French onion soup, Provençal tomato soup, spaghetti sauce, chicken stews like paprika chicken, and fish soups such as bouillabaisse. Being antimicrobial and antioxidant, it is a healthy addition.

Bay leaves are easily bought in stores, but also readily dried, if you have a tree. The leaves dry quickly, since they are flat and not very thick. August is recommended as the best time to harvest a lot of them from an outdoor tree. You can also freeze the leaves to preserve them. Bay leaves are often used fresh. Fresh or frozen bay leaves have a stronger flavor than dried ones, but most recipes assume dried bay leaves. When cooking with fresh or frozen bay leaves, use fewer than the recipe calls for. But one of the joys of growing bay as an evergreen plant or a houseplant is that there are fresh leaves all year.

In the United States today, if you buy dry bay leaves from a grocery store, they are almost always Grecian bay imported from Turkey, Algeria, or southern Europe. If the store offers you fresh bay leaves, they are usually California bay. This is another reason why fresh bay leaves aren't quite the same as dry bay leaves.

Bay leaves should be fished out of the food and not eaten. They are not poisonous. Their reputation as poisonous probably was borrowed from the similar-shaped leaves of cherry laurel, which are quite toxic. The actual reason not to eat the bay leaves in the stew is because they are so stiff. Hours of cooking won't make them soft, so you risk of scratching your mouth or throat if you swallow them. Leave the leaf in the bowl.

A time-honored way to cook with bay is to use a bouquet garni. The bouquet garni is a bundle of dry herbs prepared in advance, usually in a mesh bag. The spices vary but generally include bay, cloves, peppercorns, and dried leafy herbs such as parsley and thyme. The cook tosses the bouquet garni into the soup or stew, then removes it before serving the dish.

Grilling over bay wood imparts the intriguing scent of bay to meats and shellfish. Bay wood for grilling is not generally available, but much the same effect can be produced by adding bay leaves to the fire just before grilling.

A lovely herb from a pretty plant, bay is an herb I strongly recommend.

⤖ Traditional Spaghetti and Meatballs

As a newlywed in 1945, my mother copied this recipe from Italian friends in New York City. We modified it over the years.

For the meatballs:

> 1 pound ground beef (or bison)
>
> 1 slice bread soaked with water and then wrung out
>
> 1 grated onion
>
> 1 tablespoon dried parsley
>
> Dash of poultry seasoning
>
> Dash of powdered sage
>
> Pepper
>
> Salt if desired
>
> ¼–½ cup salad oil

For the sauce:

> 1 onion, thinly sliced (note: this is the second onion used)
>
> 1 clove of garlic, quartered
>
> 1 28-ounce jar of whole, peeled tomatoes
>
> 1–2 5.3-ounce tubes of tomato paste
>
> ½ cup water (or more)
>
> 1–2 bay leaves
>
> 4–5 cloves (if using powdered cloves, use about ½ teaspoon)
>
> 7-ounce package of spaghetti, cooked according to directions on package

Combine meat, bread, onion, parsley, poultry seasoning, sage, pepper, and salt and mix well. Form into 1-inch meatballs. Cook in a skillet in salad oil until brown. Remove from the skillet.

To start the sauce, add onion and garlic to the skillet and sauté in the drippings until yellow. Add tomatoes, tomato paste, ½ cup of water, bay leaves, and cloves. For a thinner sauce, add more water. Simmer 1½ hours, and 30 minutes before serving, return the meatballs to the sauce. Cover and cook slowly. Pour over spaghetti. Serves 4–5.

☙ Split Pea Soup

Also a traditional recipe of my family, this split pea soup serves 4–6.

You will need:

> 1 carrot
>
> 1 small onion
>
> 1 cup dry split peas
>
> Cooked ham bone (or 1 slice cooked bacon or 1 table-spoon toasted sesame oil)
>
> 1 bay leaf
>
> 5 cups water

Chop the carrot and onion. Simmer all ingredients together, covered, for 2 hours or until the peas are tender. Remove ham bone (or bacon piece) and bay leaf. Blend it in a blender (taking care not to burn yourself) or push it through a sieve for a uniform texture. Serve hot.

Resource

Culpeper, Nicholas. *The Complete Herbal*. London: Thomas Kelly, 1835. Page 18.

Summer Savory

～ Marilyn I. Bellemore ～

Though William Shakespeare wrote, "Here's flowers for you: / Hot lavender, mints, savory, marjoram" in *The Winter's Tale*, published in 1623, the origins of savory to flavor food can be traced back more than two thousand years.

Summer savory and winter savory are cooking herbs, and my focus is on the former, popular in the cuisine of Atlantic Canada. My interest in summer savory (called *sarriette* in French) began as I learned more about my Acadian heritage. The Acadians were descendants of the French who settled in Acadia, what is now Eastern Canada's Maritime provinces and parts of Quebec, modern-day Maine to the Kennebec

Summer Savory	
Species	*Satureja hortensis*
Zone	1 to 11, as an annual
Needs	☀️☀️☀️ 💧💧💧
Soil pH	6.8 to 7.0
Size	18" tall

River, and the west coast of Newfoundland during the seventeenth and eighteenth centuries.

Summer savory is used in delicious Acadian dishes such as *fricot* (a meat and potato stew); *rapure* (affectionately called "rappie pie"), generally a mixture of chicken and potatoes; and also bread stuffing for turkey on Thanksgiving Day, celebrated in October in Eastern Canada and the Maritimes.

When I visited my paternal grandmother's birthplace of Prince Edward Island (PEI) in 2019 as an adult, I was thrilled to taste fresh summer savory for the first time in many restaurants. I had tried unsuccessfully to find the herb either fresh or dried in supermarkets and specialty stores when I was living in Vermont. Although nothing compares to summer savory fresh from the garden, on PEI I was able to buy a jar of the dried herb and cook with it primarily during the winter months.

It is so popular in Canada that in 2017 the Albert County Museum in Hopewell Cape, New Brunswick, hosted a lecture on how to grow summer savory and made a tasty meal of fricot for participants as part of the Growing Together project, celebrating Canada's 150th year through food, seeds, and stories.

Growing Summer Savory

An annual, the herb is planted from seed and in early spring is sown directly in the garden. Summer savory also thrives as a container plant to keep on your windowsill. The herb needs full sunlight and extra watering. When planting the seeds, keep them twelve to eighteen inches apart and be sure not to cover them with soil. Simply press the seed with your fingertip into the ground.

*Vesey Seeds in York, PEI, sells summer savory seeds for a
modest price in its seed catalogue and online.*

Summer savory is ready to pick between July and October.
You can cut the leaves off, and the herb will continue to grow
as long as you don't cut down to the base of the stalk. Much
like lettuce, the more you cut the more it will grow. As a general rule, don't harvest until the stalks are around seven inches
in height.

The plant is very aromatic. The stems are bushy and hairy
with pointed narrow leaves that are dark green in color. In late
summer, they bloom flowers that range from a white or pale
pink color to a pretty lavender.

Cooking with Summer Savory

Summer savory is native to the Mediterranean. Interestingly
enough, I've never tasted it in Italian cooking. It is included in
herbes de Provence, named for the region of France, an aromatic
mixture of dried herbs and spices that includes summer and
winter savory, thyme, basil, rosemary, tarragon, marjoram,
oregano, and bay leaf. When the European colonists brought
summer savory to the Maritime provinces, it adapted nicely,
thus becoming sturdier, more flavorful, and with a stronger
fragrance. Some people think summer savory tastes mild compared to the perennial winter savory. Personally, I think it has a
kick to it with its peppery taste.

One proposed etymology for savory's genus, *Satureja*, is
from the word "satyr," a half-man, half-goat creature (ears,

legs, horns, and tail) that lurked in ancient mythological Roman forests. Roman writer Pliny called it an aphrodisiac, so it was used abundantly in Roman cooking. The Roman poet Virgil attested that planting savory near beehives made the honey taste more flavorful and delicious, shares Maryann Readall for the Herb Society of America. The Egyptians loved it too! They powdered the herb to create love potions, to aid sore throats, and treat bee stings.

Summer savory is often used to flavor meats. Before becoming a vegetarian, my Acadian cousin Corinne made many recipes with the herb. Once she stopped eating meat, she said her foods just didn't taste as good as they used to. Corinne learned to incorporate summer savory into her cooking, and that solved the problem of flavorless dinners!

Luckily, summer savory pairs well with beans. In addition to improving their taste, it helps prevents the flatulence that is a common occurrence when eating them. I had to laugh when I read this quote from seventeenth-century herbalist John Gerard's *The Herball, or Generall History of Plantes* about the wonders of summer savory: "It maketh thin, and doth maruellously preuaile against winde [gas]: therefore it is with good successe boiled and eaten with beanes, peason, and other windie pulses."

Acadian Recipes

The following authentic Acadian recipes were given to me by family and friends on PEI. True comfort food, they were passed down through generations with a bit of tweaking here and there.

✎ Cousin Roma's Chicken Fricot

The first time I tried chicken fricot (chicken stew) was in the late 1970s at an Acadian restaurant called Etoile de Mer in Mont-Carmel, PEI. I was with my family visiting my paternal grandmother's ancestral home, and part of the journey was tasting the foods that had been a part of her everyday life. It takes a little over an hour to prepare and serves 4. Many families serve this dish with dumplings.

You will need:

2–3 pounds of boneless, skinless chicken cut into pieces

1 peeled and chopped onion

1 tablespoon butter

1–2 cups fresh chicken broth

6 peeled and cubed potatoes

2 teaspoons chopped fresh summer savory

Salt and pepper to taste

In a frying pan, brown the chicken and onion in butter. Transfer to a cooking pot. Add the chicken broth and then water to cover. Simmer for 30 minutes.

Add the potatoes and summer savory, and simmer until the potatoes are cooked. Add salt and pepper to taste.

✎ Cousin Leona's Acadian Rapure

Rapure is an Acadian dish popular on PEI and in southwest Nova Scotia. Rapure's origins are thought to be the Acadian Expulsion (in the mid-eighteenth century, the British forcibly removed the Acadian people from the modern-day Maritime provinces and Maine, resulting in the loss of thousands of lives).

You will need:

- 1 pound cubed pork
- ½ cup vegetable oil
- 1 large onion, diced
- 10 pounds potatoes
- Salt and pepper to taste
- 1 teaspoon chopped fresh summer savory
- 1 teaspoon coriander powder (optional)
- 1 teaspoon of baking soda dissolved in ¼ cup hot water
- 1 egg
- 2 cups dried bread crumbs

Preheat your oven to 400°F.

Cook the pork in ½ cup vegetable oil. Add the onion and cook for 15 more minutes. Peel and boil 2 large potatoes, then mash them and add them to the pork mixture. Transfer the mixture to a bowl and set aside.

Peel, wash, and grate the remainder of the potatoes. Grate them under running hot water so they don't turn brown. When finished, wash the potatoes well in cold water to remove the starch. Now put them in a fine strainer or cheese cloth to remove excess water.

Transfer the grated potatoes to a large bowl and mix all together with the pork mixture and the remaining ingredients. Put in a 13 × 9-inch pan. Bake at 400°F for 1 hour, then lower the temperature to 350°F and bake for another hour or until nicely golden.

❧ Corilyn Azaelia's Bread Stuffing

My Canadian friend Corilyn gave me this recipe. As with many stuffings, this one does not follow a written recipe. It's based solely on taste and the amount of people being served. I still think it's worth sharing because summer savory really shines through in the taste of a stuffed turkey or chicken.

Crumble crusty bread into a bowl. Add chopped fresh summer savory along with chopped garlic and onion. Moisten the mixture with water or beef, chicken, or vegetable broth. Add salt and pepper to taste. Stuff your turkey or chicken, put it in the oven, and cook according to the bird's weight.

❧ Marilyn's Tourtière

This is my own version of the French Canadian / Acadian meat pie popular at Christmastime and New Year's Eve.

You will need:

1 pound ground pork

1 pound ground beef or shredded chicken

½ onion

¼ teaspoon allspice

¼ teaspoon ground cloves

¼ teaspoon dry summer savory

8 ounces water

1 large potato, boiled then mashed

1 box refrigerated pie crust

Preheat oven to 425°F. In a saucepan, combine all ingredients except the potato and pie crust. Cook over medium heat until the mixture boils, stirring occasionally. Reduce heat to low and simmer until the meat is cooked, about 5 minutes. Remove from heat and mix in the potato.

Place the pie crust in a 9-inch pie pan. Spoon the meat mixture into the pie crust. Place the top crust on top of the pie and pinch the edges to seal. Cut slits in the top crust so steam can escape. Cover the edges of the pie with strips of aluminum foil.

Cook at 425°F for 35 minutes or until the crust is golden. Let cool 5 minutes before slicing.

Resources

Gerard, John. *The Herball, or Generall History of Plantes.* London: John Norton, 1597. Page 462.

Kowalchik, Claire, and Wiliam H. Hylton, eds. *Rodale's Illustrated Encyclopedia of Herbs.* Emmaus, PA: Rodale Press, 1987.

Readall, Maryann. "Summer Savory—Herb of the Month." The Herb Society of America. July 5, 2021. https://herbsocietyblog .wordpress.com/2021/07/05/summer-savory-herb-of-the -month/.

Shakespeare, William. *The Winter's Tale.* Folger Shakespeare Library. Act 4, scene 4, line 125. https://www.folger.edu/winters-tale.

Smith, Miranda. *Your Backyard Herb Garden.* Emmaus, PA: Rodale Press, 1997.

Elderberry

⇝ Jordan Charbonneau ⇜

Friend to people, birds, bees, and streams, the humble elderberry has a lot going for it. I love seeing it in bloom, gracing damp roadsides with its delicate sprays of tiny white flowers. Various pollinators share my love for its blossoms, and when the flowers give way to fruit, you'll often find these drooping shrubs covered in songbirds. You might also see birds headed to and from elderberry patches in spring. Their dense growth habit provides excellent nesting habitat for birds. Bumblebees also utilize it for nesting, preferring its hollow stems for laying their eggs. The elderberry's impressive root systems and high tolerance for moisture lend the plant to erosion prevention in rain gardens and on stream banks.

Elderberry	
Species	*Sambucus canadensis*
Zone	3–9
Needs	☀ 🌢🌢
Soil pH	5.5–6.5
Size	5–12 ft. tall

Humans have also utilized elderberries for at least four thousand years! Their flowers and berries are food and a potent herbal remedy. While the rest of the stems and leaves are poisonous for consumption, humans have also used the wood for crafting tools, toys, and instruments for centuries.

There are species of elderberry native to regions all over the world. The one you're most likely to find in North America is the American black elderberry (*Sambucus canadensis*), also known as American elder, common elderberry, or just elder. This helpful shrub grows five to twelve feet tall with loose branches bearing pinnately compound leaves. The leaves are made up of four to ten pairs of ovate to elliptical leaflets.

You'll typically spot elderberries growing in moist areas such as along stream banks and roadside ditches and in moist woodlands and thickets. Elderberry stands out more when in flower or fruit. The tiny lemon-scented flowers bloom in June and July and form flat-topped clusters up to ten inches across. The flowers produce clusters of small dark purple to black fruits in late summer. Those in the Southeastern United States should take care not to confuse these with the dark berries of poisonous American pokeweed (*Phytolacca americana*).

You may also spot European elder (*Sambucus nigra*) in cultivation or naturalized around old farms and homesteads. European elder is more tree-like than its American cousin, growing eight to twenty feet tall. You can use its flowers and berries just as you would those of the American elderberry.

Growing Elderberry

Elderberry bushes are commercially available today at many nurseries; however, they can be pricey. Thankfully, they're also easy to propagate from cuttings. I've propagated plants for my homestead by taking cuttings from a large patch of plants growing on a nearby roadside. Just remember to get the landowner's permission.

Take cuttings in the winter when the plants have gone dormant. Use sharp shears that you've sterilized with rubbing alcohol. Cuttings should be six to eight inches long from a branch that's about the same size as a pencil in diameter. The branch should be free from signs of disease and damage. You only want healthy plants! Cut the bottom at a 45-degree angle and the top straight so that you know which is the top. Trust me—this will save you a lot of time.

Soak your cuttings in water for twenty-four hours; a quart-size mason jar works well for this. While they're soaking, prepare small pots or trays of potting soil. You can even use old yogurt containers for this. Using your finger, make a hole in the soil about one to two inches deep for each of your cuttings.

After twenty-four hours, dip the bottom end of each cutting in rooting hormone powder; this should be available at most garden supply stores. Place each cutting in a hole and gently pack the soil around it. Keep your cutting somewhere between 40 and 50 degrees Fahrenheit and out of direct wind and sunlight for about eight to ten weeks. I used our root cellar, but an unheated basement or garage may also work well for this. Keep the soil moist during this time but not soggy.

After this time, your cuttings should have formed roots! You should now pot up your new elderberry plants into slightly larger containers. Wait to transplant them outdoors until all danger of frost has passed.

While elderberry is quite hardy and will tolerate a wide range of soils, it thrives in moist, slightly acidic soil. Loamy soil is best, but it will tolerate clay soils, particularly if there's good drainage. You should select an area that has full sun to partial shade. If you're growing it in full sun, you may need to water more frequently.

Elderberries make excellent hedges or additions to rain gardens. They're also a great native choice for helping stabilize stream banks. When selecting a planting site, consider that they spread through root rhizomes. To prevent them from spreading, you'll need to keep on top of pruning them back.

Plant your elderberries in the spring after the danger of frost has passed. Digging your hole larger than it needs to be and filling in around your elderberry's roots with well-aged compost can help the plant get established. You may also want to consider pinching off any flowers the first year. This encourages the plant to put more energy into root growth.

Elderberry in History

Human history is laced with our interactions with plants. Elderberry has long been one of humankind's strong allies. Scientists have found elderberry seeds in Neolithic dwellings in Switzerland that date back to 2000 BCE! Other cultures around the world also used elderberries. It is also believed that receding glaciers deposited the seeds in Asia, Europe, and America around 9000 BCE.

As a medicinal plant, the elderberry has been listed in various historical texts. Pliny the Elder, Dioscorides, John Gerard, and Nicholas Culpeper, famous physicians dating from 77 CE to the mid-1600s, all mention elderberries in their writings. Native Americans were reportedly using elderberries to treat various conditions at the time of contact with settlers. The settlers also brought their traditional uses of the plant from England, where it was known as "nature's medicine chest" or "the medicine chest of the country people." Using elderberries today is an excellent way to connect with these age-old traditions.

Beyond food and medicine, the wood was useful for tools and crafts. The pith at the center of the elder stem is easy to remove and makes an excellent blowing tube for kindling fire. The scientific name *Sambucas* is derived from the Greek *sambuca*, a stringed instrument made from elder wood.

The wood polished easily and was also used to make needles for weaving nets, toys, skewers, pegs for shoemakers, flutes, and other instruments.

Elderberry in the Kitchen

The tiny dark berries don't seem like a top choice for sweet treats. Raw, they're terrible tasting and toxic. Thankfully, with a bit of cooking, elderberries are tasty and perfect for a myriad of recipes. You can add them to pies, crisps, jams, chutneys, and jellies. The juice also makes delicious popsicles perfect for kids (or adults!) with sore throats.

To preserve whole berries, you can freeze them in airtight containers or dry them in your dehydrator. Just make sure you dry them until they're completely dry and crisp to prevent mold. Store dried berries in an airtight container out of direct sunlight.

The flowers are also a wonderful addition to several recipes. You can dip them in batter and fry them into fritters, steep them as tea, or add them to tinctures and salves. To preserve elderflowers, dry them in a dehydrator on low or your "herb" setting. Store dried elderflowers in an airtight container out of direct sunlight.

⚜ Elderberry Syrup

My favorite use for elderberries is straightforward elderberry syrup. The syrup can be used simply for its sweet flavor or as an herbal remedy. It's a fun ingredient to add to cocktails or lemonade for get-togethers. I love adding other medicinal herbs to mine and taking it during the fall as a preventative against colds and flus. Elderberries are high in minerals and vitamins, especially vitamin C. They also have potent antiviral properties, making elderberry syrup a common choice for treating colds, the flu, and coughs.

The optional ingredients can be added to your syrup to give it an extra medicinal boost. You can also decrease the amount of sugar or honey, but it will be thinner and won't keep as well. It's a great recipe to experiment with and find what works best for you.

You will need:

6 cups fresh elderberries (or 3 cups dried elderberries)

6 cups water

3 cups raw honey (replace with sugar or maple syrup for a vegan option)

Optional ingredients:

1 tablespoon dried echinacea root (anti-inflammatory, immune-boosting, not a great flavor)

1 tablespoon grated ginger (helps settle upset stomachs)

2 cinnamon sticks (anti-inflammatory)

1 tablespoon dried licorice root (especially good for sore throats)

12 tablespoons dried rose hips (extra vitamin C)

Peel from an organic orange or lemon (extra vitamin C and nice flavor)

Large pot

Fine strainer or cloth (optional)

Clean jars or bottles

The most tedious part of this recipe is separating the berries from the stems. Once you've separated the berries, you'll want to boil them with the water and any of the optional herbs and spices of your choosing. Don't add your sweetener just yet! Simmer your mixture gently for 45 to 60 minutes or until about half of the water is gone. Then strain your mixture, composting any of the solids. If you're using honey or maple syrup, you can stir it in once the mixture has cooled to about room temperature. Don't heat your raw honey, as this destroys all the healthful enzymes!

If you're using sugar, you may want to bring your mixture back to a simmer while you stir it in. This helps ensure that the sugar fully dissolves.

Store your syrup in clean glass jars or bottles. This recipe will keep about 1 month in the fridge or can be frozen to last all winter.

Adults should take 2 teaspoons every 3 hours when they begin to feel sick and can continue for the duration of an illness. Children should take 1–2 teaspoons twice per day.

Note that this recipe isn't intended to be medical advice. Raw honey can be dangerous to children under the age of 1.

⤜ Elderflower Champagne

Who doesn't love champagne? While this recipe technically isn't champagne as it doesn't include grapes from the Champagne region of France, it is a delicious local alternative. I can't think of a better way to celebrate summer than with something made from local flowers.

You'll need a bit of patience, as this recipe has to ferment for several weeks. Don't let the word *ferment* scare you, though; this recipe is simple and safe to make, even for the complete beginner. It makes about 1 gallon.

You will need:

8–10 large elderberry flower clusters

1 pound honey or 1½ pounds sugar

4 cups filtered, unchlorinated water (chlorine can kill the yeast), plus 12 cups

Peel from 1 lemon

½ teaspoon baking yeast

Pot

Large mixing bowl or additional pot

Fine mesh colander or muslin cloth for straining

Funnel

Flip-top bottles, 8–10 if using 16-ounce bottles

To get started, remove the elderberry flowers from the stems. Just like in our syrup recipe with the berries, this will be the most tedious step. Don't wash the flowers. Their natural yeast will help the champagne ferment. Next, bring 4 cups of the water to a boil. While the water is heating, place your honey or sugar in a large mixing bowl or pot (it will need to fit all the ingredients). Pour your boiling water over the honey or sugar and lemon peel, stirring until the sugar or honey is fully dissolved.

Then stir in the remaining 12 cups of cold water followed by the elderberry flowers and ½ teaspoon of yeast. Cover this mixture with a clean dish towel and let it sit for 48 hours, stirring at least twice per day.

After 2 days, you should see signs of fermentation. The liquid should be bubbly and may have a layer of foam on the top.

Pour your champagne through a fine mesh colander or muslin cloth to remove any solids and transfer it to flip-top glass bottles, leaving at least 1 inch of headspace. I can often find these at thrift stores or garage sales, but they can also be purchased online or at brewery supply stores. Don't use corked bottles; the pressure from the fermentation will push the corks out.

Leave your bottles of champagne at room temperature but out of direct sunlight for 1 week. You'll need to "burp" the bottles once daily, opening the caps to let off the pressure. If you forget this step, the bottles can become too pressurized and explode.

Then, you can move them to a refrigerator or a root cellar. Continue burping them for an additional week; fermentation should begin to slow down during this time. After a week of storing them somewhere cool, you should be able to discontinue burping them. Now your champagne is ready to use! You can also keep it for several months in the fridge or cellar.

Serve your elderberry flower champagne chilled. It's the perfect beverage for garden parties!

Resources

Brobst, J. E. "Essential Facts for Elderberry." The Herb Society of America. 2013. https://www.herbsociety.org/file_download /inline/2084e920-b3bf-48da-8596-037fd76e46b7.

Lowenstein, David, and Jeannie Nichols. "Growing Elderberry in the Garden." Michigan State University Extension. Last modified January 27, 2020. https://www.canr.msu.edu/news/elderberries _an_edible_landscape_plant.

"Sambucus canadensis." Missouri Botanical Garden. Accessed October 21, 2021. https://www.missouribotanicalgarden.org /PlantFinder/PlantFinderDetails.aspx?kempercode=f470.

"Sambucus nigra." North Carolina Cooperative Extension. Accessed October 20, 2021. https://plants.ces.ncsu.edu/plants/sambucus -nigra/.

White, Joyce. "Elderberries." Maine Organic Farmers and Gardeners. Spring 2008. https://www.mofga.org/resources/elderberries /elderberries/.

Gardening
Resources

Companion Planting Guide

Group together plants that complement each other by deterring certain pests, absorbing different amounts of nutrients from the soil, shading their neighbors, and enhancing friends' flavors. This table of herbs and common garden vegetables offers suggestions for plants to pair together and plants to keep separated.

Plant	Good Pairing	Poor Pairing
Anise	Coriander	Carrot, basil, rue
Asparagus	Tomato, parsley, basil, lovage, Asteraceae spp.	
Basil	Tomato, peppers, oregano, asparagus	Rue, sage, anise
Beans	Tomato, carrot, cucumber, cabbage, corn, cauliflower, potato	Gladiola, fennel, *Allium* spp.
Bee balm	Tomato, echinacea, yarrow, catnip	
Beet	Onions, cabbage, lettuce, mint, catnip, kohlrabi, lovage	Pole bean, field mustard
Bell pepper	Tomato, eggplant, coriander, basil	Kohlrabi
Borage	Tomato, squash, strawberry	
Broccoli	Aromatics, beans, celery, potato, onion, oregano, pennyroyal, dill, sage, beet	Tomato, pole bean, strawberry, peppers
Cabbage	Mint, sage, thyme, tomato, chamomile, hyssop, pennyroyal, dill, rosemary, sage	Strawberry, grape, tomato
Carrot	Peas, lettuce, chive, radish, leek, onion, sage, rosemary, tomato	Dill, anise, chamomile

Plant	Good Pairing	Poor Pairing
Catnip	Bee balm, cucumber, chamomile, mint	
Celery	Leek, tomato, bush bean, cabbage, cauliflower, carrot, garlic	Lovage
Chamomile	Peppermint, beans, peas, onion, cabbage, cucumber, catnip, dill, tomato, pumpkin, squash	
Chervil	Radish, lettuce, broccoli	
Chive	Carrot, *Brassica* spp., tomato, parsley	Bush bean, potato, peas, soybean
Coriander/ cilantro	*Plant anywhere*	Fennel
Corn	Potato, beans, peas, melon, squash, pumpkin, sunflower, soybean, cucumber	Quack grass, wheat, straw, tomato
Cucumber	Beans, cabbage, radish, sunflower, lettuce, broccoli, squash, corn, peas, leek, nasturtium, onion	Aromatic herbs, sage, potato, rue
Dill	Cabbage, lettuce, onion, cucumber	Carrot, caraway, tomato
Echinacea	Bee balm	
Eggplant	Catnip, green beans, lettuce, kale, redroot pigweed	
Fennel	*Isolate; disliked by all garden plants*	
Garlic	Tomato, rose	Beans, peas
Hyssop	*Most plants*	Radish
Kohlrabi	Green bean, onion, beet, cucumber	Tomato, strawberry, pole bean
Lavender	*Plant anywhere*	
Leek	Onion, celery, carrot, celeriac	Bush bean, soy bean, pole bean, pea

Plant	Good Pairing	Poor Pairing
Lemon balm	*All vegetables*, particularly squash, pumpkin	
Lettuce	Strawberry, cucumber, carrot, radish, dill	Pole bean, tomato
Lovage	*Most plants*, especially cucumber, beans, beet, *Brassica* spp., onion, leek, potato, tomato	Celery
Marjoram	*Plant anywhere*	
Melon	Corn, peas, morning glory	Potato, gourd
Mint	Cabbage, tomato, nettle	Parsley, rue
Nasturtium	Cabbage, cucumber, potato, pumpkin, radish	
Onion	Beets, chamomile, carrot, lettuce, strawberry, tomato, kohlrabi, summer savory	Peas, beans, sage
Oregano	*Most plants*	
Parsley	Tomato, asparagus, carrot, onion, rose	Mint, *Allium* spp.
Parsnip	Peas	
Peas	Radish, carrot, corn, cucumbers, bean, tomato, spinach, turnip, aromatic herbs	*Allium* spp., gladiola
Potato	Beans, corn, peas, cabbage, eggplant, catnip, horseradish, watermelon, nasturtium, flax	Pumpkin, raspberry, sunflower, tomato, orach, black walnut, cucumber, squash
Pumpkin	Corn, lemon balm	Potato
Radish	Peas, lettuce, nasturtium, chervil, cucumber	Hyssop
Rose	Rue, tomato, garlic, parsley, tansy	*Any plant within 1 ft. radius*
Rosemary	Rue, sage	

Plant	Good Pairing	Poor Pairing
Sage	Rosemary	Rue, onion
Spinach	Strawberry, garlic	
Squash	Nasturtium, corn, mint, catnip, radish, borage, lemon balm	Potato
Strawberry	Borage, bush bean, spinach, rue, lettuce	*Brassica* spp., garlic, kohlrabi
Tarragon	*Plant anywhere*	
Thyme	*Plant anywhere*	
Tomato	Asparagus, parsley, chive, onion, carrot, marigold, nasturtium, bee balm, nettle, garlic, celery, borage	Black walnut, dill, fennel, potato, *Brassica* spp., corn
Turnip	Peas, beans, brussels sprout, leek	Potato, tomato
Yarrow	*Plant anywhere*, especially with medicinal herbs	

For more information on companion planting, you may wish to consult the following resources:

Mayer, Dale. *The Complete Guide to Companion Planting: Everything You Need to Know to Make Your Garden Successful.* Ocala, FL: Atlantic Publishing, 2010.

Philbrick, Helen. *Companion Plants and How to Use Them.* Edinburgh, UK: Floris Books, 2016.

Riotte, Louise. *Carrots Love Tomatoes: Secrets of Companion Planting for Successful Gardening.* Pownal, VT: Storey Books, 1988.

Cooking with Herbs and Spices

Elevate your cooking with herbs and spices. Remember, a little goes a long way!

Herb	Flavor Pairings	Health Benefits
Anise	Salads, slaws, roasted vegetables	Reduces nausea, gas, and bloating. May relieve infant colic. May help menstrual pain. Loosens sputum in respiratory illnesses.
Basil	Pesto and other pasta sauces, salads	Eases stomach cramps, nausea, indigestion, and colic. Mild sedative action.
Borage	Soups	Soothes respiratory congestion. Eases sore, inflamed skin. Mild diuretic properties.
Cayenne	Adds a spicy heat to soups, sauces, and main courses	Stimulates blood flow. Relieves joint and muscle pain. Treats gas and diarrhea.
Chamomile	Desserts, teas	Used for nausea, indigestion, gas pains, bloating, and colic. Relaxes tense muscles. Eases menstrual cramps. Promotes relaxation and sleep.
Chervil	Soups, salads, and sauces	Settles and supports digestion. Mild diuretic properties. Useful in treating minor skin irritations.
Chive	Salads, potato dishes, sauces	Rich in antioxidants. May benefit insomnia. Contributes to strong bones.
Coriander/ cilantro	Soups, picante sauces, salsas	Treats mild digestive disorders. Counters nervous tensions. Sweetens breath.

Herb	Flavor Pairings	Health Benefits
Dill	Cold salads and fish dishes	Treats all types of digestive disorders, including colic. Sweetens breath. Mild diuretic.
Echinacea	Teas	Supports immune function. May treat or prevent infection.
Fennel	Salads, stir-fry, vegetable dishes	Settles stomach pain, relieves bloating, and stimulates appetite. May help treat kidney stones and bladder infections. Mild expectorant. Eye wash treats conjunctivitis.
Garlic	All types of meat and vegetable dishes as well as soup stocks and bone broths	Antiseptic: aids in wound healing. Treats and may prevent infections. Benefits the heart and circulatory system.
Ginger	Chicken, pork, stir-fry, gingerbread and ginger cookies	Treats all types of digestive disorders. Stimulates circulation. Soothes colds and flu.
Hyssop	Chicken, pasta sauces, light soups	Useful in treating respiratory problems and bronchitis. Expectorant. Soothes the digestive tract.
Jasmine	Chicken dishes, fruit desserts	Relieves tension and provides mild sedation. May be helpful in depression. Soothes dry or sensitive skin.
Lavender	Chicken, fruit dishes, ice cream	Soothes and calms the nerves. Relieves indigestion, gas, and colic. May relax airways in asthma.

Herb	Flavor Pairings	Health Benefits
Lemon balm	Soups, sauces, seafood dishes	Soothes and calms the nerves. Treats mild anxiety and depression. Helps heal wounds.
Lemon-grass	Marinades, stir-fries, curries, spice rubs	Treats all types of digestive disorders. Reduces fever. May reduce pain.
Lemon verbena	Beverages, any recipe asking for lemon zest	Calms digestive problems and treats stomach pain. Gently sedative.
Lovage	Soups, lovage pesto, lentils	Acts as a digestive and respiratory tonic. Has diuretic and antimicrobial actions. Boosts circulation. Helps menstrual pain.
Marigold	Soups, salads, rice dishes	Effective treatment of minor wounds, insect bites, sunburn, acne, and other skin irritations. Benefits menstrual pain and excessive bleeding.
Marjoram	Vegetables, soups, tomato dishes, sausages	Calms the digestive system. Stimulates appetite.
Nasturtium	Nasturtium pesto, salad dressings, salads	Strong antibiotic properties. Treats wounds and respiratory infections.
Oregano	Chicken, tomato sauces and dishes	Strong antiseptic properties. Stimulates bile production. Eases flatulence.
Parsley	Soups, stocks, bone broths	Highly nutritious. Strong diuretic action and may help treat cystitis. Benefits gout, rheumatism, and arthritis.
Peppermint	Desserts, teas	Treats all types of digestive disorders. May help headaches.

Herb	Flavor Pairings	Health Benefits
Purslane	Salads	Treats digestive and bladder ailments. Mild antibiotic effects.
Rosemary	Roasted red meats, potato dishes, grilled foods	Stimulates circulation. May stimulate the adrenal glands. Elevates mood and may benefit depression.
Sage	Chicken, duck, and pork	Relieves pain in sore throats. May help treat menstrual and menopausal disorders.
Spinach	Sautéed, soups, salads, spinach pesto, stuffed in chicken, ravioli	Iron-rich; supports healthy blood and iron stores.
Summer savory	Mushrooms, vegetables, quiche	Treats digestive and respiratory issues.
Tarragon	Chicken, fish, vegetables, sauces—"classic French cooking"	Stimulates digestion. Promotes sleep—mildly sedative. Induces menstruation.
Thyme	Soups, stews, tomato-based sauces	May treat infections. Soothes sore throats and hay fever. Can help expel parasites. Relieves minor skin irritations.
Wintergreen	Ice cream, candies, desserts	Strong anti-inflammatory and antiseptic properties. Treats arthritis and rheumatism. Relieves flatulence.
Winter savory	Beans, meats, vegetables	Treats digestive and respiratory issues. Antibacterial properties.
Yarrow	Salad dressings, infused oils	Helps heal minor wounds. Eases menstrual pain and heavy flow. Tonic properties.

Gardening Techniques

Gardeners are creative people who are always on the lookout for the most efficient, interesting, and beautiful ways to grow their favorite plants. Whether you need to save money, reduce your workload, or keep plants indoors, the following gardening techniques are just a sampling of the many ways to grow your very own bountiful garden.

Barrel

Lidless plastic food-grade barrels or drums are set on raised supports. Before the barrel is filled with soil, slits are cut into the sides of the barrel and shaped into pockets. A PVC pipe is perforated with holes and set into the center and out of the bottom of the barrel as a delivery tool for watering, draining, fertilizing, and feeding the optional worm farm.

Strengths
Initial cost is moderate. Retains moisture, warms quickly, drains well, takes up little space, maximizes growing area, and repels burrowing rodents. Little weeding or back-bending required.

Weaknesses
Not always attractive, initially labor intensive, requires special tools to modify. Not generally suited for crops that are deep-rooted, large vining, or traditionally grown in rows, such as corn.

Hügelkultur

These permanent raised beds utilize decomposing logs and woody brush that have been stacked into a pyramidal form on top of the soil's surface or in shallow trenches and then packed and covered with eight to ten inches of soil, compost, and well-rotted manure. The rotting wood encourages soil biota while holding and releasing moisture to plants, much like a sponge. English pronunciation: "hoogle-culture."

Strengths
Vertical form warms quickly, drains well, reduces watering needs, increases overall planting surface, and reduces bending chores. In time the rotting wood breaks down into humus-rich soil.

Weaknesses
Labor-intensive construction and mulch tends to slide down sides. Requires two to three years of nitrogen supplementation, repeated soaking, and filling sunken voids with soil. Voids can also be attractive to rodents and snakes in the first few years.

Hydroponic

Hydroponics is based on a closed (greenhouse) system relying on carefully timed circulation of nutrient-enriched water flowing through a soilless growing medium in which plants grow. Aerial parts are supported above the water by rafts and, at times, vertical supports. With the addition of fish tanks to the system, hydroponics becomes aquaponics.

Strengths
Customizable to any size. Versatile, efficient, productive, and weedless. Produce stays clean.

Weaknesses

Large systems are expensive and complicated to set up and maintain; require multiple inputs of heat, light, and nutrients; and are limited to certain crop types.

Lasagna

Based on sheet composting, lasagna gardens are built up in layers, starting with paper or cardboard that is placed on top of turf-covered or tilled ground to smother weeds and feed ground worm activity. This is then covered in repeating layers of peat moss, compost, leaves, wood chips, manure, and yard waste (green, brown, green), which eventually break down into rich, humusy soil.

Strengths

Excellent natural method to enrich poor soils, utilizes organic waste, supports soil biota, and improves drainage while reducing the need for fertilizers and excessive watering.

Weaknesses

Initially labor intensive and the proper breakdown of bed materials takes months, so is not suited to "quick" gardening. Requires ready and abundant sources of clean, unsprayed, organic materials.

Ruth Stout

This "no work" garden is based on deep, permanent layers of progressively rotting straw mulch, which simultaneously builds soil, feeds plants, blocks weeds, and reduces watering. Seeds and plants are placed into the lower decomposed layers. Fresh straw is added as plants grow and kept at a depth of eight or more inches.

Strengths

No tilling, few weeds, reduced watering and fertilizing. Warms quickly in the spring and prevents winter heaving. An excellent method for rocky, sandy, or clay soils.

Weaknesses

Requires an abundance of straw each season, which can be expensive and difficult to transport, move, and store. Deep mulch may encourage burrowing rodents and provide shelter for slugs, insect pests, and diseases.

Soil Bag

This simple method utilizes one or more twenty- to forty-pound bags of commercial potting soil or topsoil simply laid out flat on turf, mulch, or wood pallets. A rectangular hole is cut into the top and drainage holes are punched through the bottom. A light dusting of fertilizer is mixed in and plants and seeds are sown.

Strengths

Super easy, weed-free, no-till garden and a great way to start an in-ground garden. Fun for kids and those without a yard.

Weaknesses

Limited to shallow-rooted crops, needs consistent watering and fertilizing, and may flood in heavy rains. Cats may find this an attractive litter box.

Straw Bale

One or more square, string-bound straw bales are placed cut side up either directly on the ground or on top of a weed barrier and soaked with water for several days or even months and treated with nitrogen to help speed the decomposition of the straw. Alternatively, bales can be overwintered in place before using. Once ready, bales are parted down the center, filled with soil and compost, and planted with seeds or starts.

Strengths

Good on poor soils, even concrete. No tilling required, few weeds, handicap accessible, versatile, easy to configure, and renter-friendly. Spent bales make excellent mulch.

Weaknesses

Straw bales can be expensive, heavy, and difficult to transport. These gardens can initially be labor intensive, require frequent watering and fertilizing, and must be replaced every one or two seasons. Nitrogen from treated bales can leach into the local environment and affect the watershed.

Square Foot

This modern take on French Intensive gardening utilizes raised beds filled with a special soilless blend enclosed in a box frame that is further divided into twelve-by-twelve-inch squares, or one square foot. Each square is planted or seeded based on the correct spacing requirements of each plant. Large crops, like tomatoes, are planted one to a square, while small crops like radishes are planted sixteen to a square.

Strengths

Proper plant spacing utilizes space, increases yields, and reduces weeds. Adding trellises increases growing capacity. Raised beds drain well, warm quickly, hold mulch, look tidy, and are easy to mow around.

Weaknesses

Initial construction is expensive, labor intensive, and often impermanent. Requires frequent watering in dry spells, and not all crops are suitable. Grids can be tedious to use and do not remove the gardener's need to learn proper plant spacing.

Vertical

Vertical gardens make use of nontraditional gardening space in two ways. The first is by training vining and climbing plants onto trellises, arbors, or fences and growing in raised beds, pots, urns, or tubs. The second is by firmly securing containers, troughs, rain gutters, or vertical garden felt pockets onto permanent frames supported by fences, walls, or other sturdy vertical structures. These gardens are typically irrigated by automatic drip or hydroponic systems. Soilless options are available.

Strengths

Attractive and weed-free indoor-outdoor garden perfect for small yards, renters, and disabled persons. Helps hide ugly structures and views and defines outdoor spaces.

Weaknesses

Construction of large systems and very sturdy structures can be initially expensive or labor intensive. Not conducive to all garden crops and requires frequent and consistent applications of moisture and fertilizer.

2023 Themed Garden Plans

Serenity Bench Garden

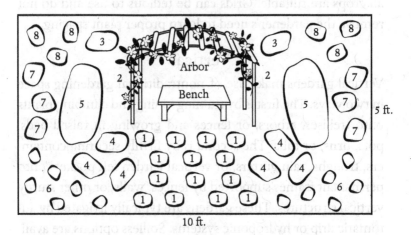

Arbor

Bench

5 ft.

10 ft.

1. Thyme (*Thymus serpyllum*), 14 sets
2. Carolina jasmine (*Gelsemium sempervirens*), 2
3. 'Sky Pencil' holly (*Ilex crenata* 'Sky Pencil'), 2
4. Lemon balm (*Melissa officinalis*), 6
5. Perilla (*Perilla frutescens*), 20
6. Golden feverfew (*Tanacetum parthenium* 'Aureum'), 12
7. Mullein (*Verbascum thapsus*), 6
8. Meadowsweet (*Filipendula ulmaria*), 6

Sometimes you need your own special spot to get away from it all. This garden features a short bench under an arbor draped with Carolina jasmine. The bench is accessed through a carpet of creeping thyme. Subtle fragrances from the remaining plants waft around the bench at different times of the year.

Tough as Nails Garden

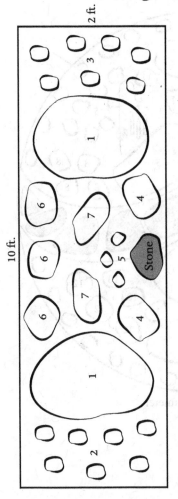

1. Dwarf mugo pine (*Pinus mugo* 'Slowmound'), 2
2. Yarrow (*Achillea millefolium*), 7 sets
3. Sea thrift (*Armeria maritima*), 7
4. Gaillardia (*Gaillardia aristata*), 6
5. Sedum (*Hylotelephium telephium* 'Herbstfreude' or 'Autumn Joy'), 3
6. Muhly grass (*Muhlenbergia capillaris*), 6
7. Anise hyssops (*Agastache foeniculum*), 2

Every landscape has that one spot that is too narrow for most bushes, too dry for most annuals and too plain to just leave alone. It might be between a sidewalk and garage. It might be down by the mailbox at the street. Or it could be some lonely strip of land between two different properties. This design is meant for a narrow bed roughly 10 feet long, but the design can be repeated for as long of a strip as needed. The stone in the center is meant to be a focal point, but the two dwarf mugo pines might steal the show as specimen plants. Be sure to specify "dwarf" mugo pine when you visit the nursery. All mugos are slow growing, but the standard mugo can eventually get 8 feet tall and 10 feet wide!

Wisdom Garden

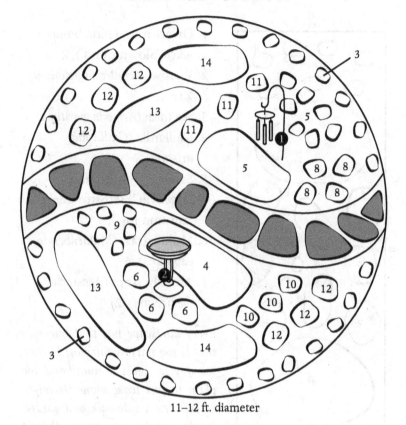

11–12 ft. diameter

1. Hanging wind chime
2. Bird bath
3. Liriope (*Liriope muscari*), 30 sets
4. Peppermint (*Mentha ×piperita*), 7
5. Spearmint (*Mentha spicata*), 7
6. Rosemary (*Salvia rosmarinus*), 3
7. Iris (*Iris germanica*), 8

8. Culinary sage (*Salvia officinalis*), 4

9. Blue sage (*Salvia azurea*), 6

10. Russian sage (*Salvia yangii*, formerly *Perovskia atriplicifolia*), 3

11. Pineapple sage (*Salvia elegans*), 3

12. Shrub cinquefoil (*Dasiphora fruticosa*, syn. *Potentilla fruticosa*), 6

13. Perennial verbena (*Glandularia canadensis*, syn. *Verbena canadensis*), 14

14. Wormwood (*Artemisia absinthium*), 4

This garden design takes its inspiration from the yin-yang symbol, the taijitu. The dot on the upper half of the circle is marked with a wind chime, hung from a shepherd's hook plant hanger. The dot in the lower half is marked with a bird bath. Rosemary and peppermint are included for anyone to stay focused and alert. The main feature of the garden is the mixture of salvias, or sages, contained herein. Although the botanical name Salvia comes from Latin meaning "to save," today people think of sage as a plant of wisdom—possibly for all the important uses for the plant. Regardless of whether you say salvia or sage, this plant is durable in the garden and beloved by bees and hummingbirds. As a gentle reminder that personal wisdom should always be evolving, there is one changeling in this design. Can you spot it?

Planning Your 2023 Garden

Prepare your soil by tilling and fertilizing. Use the grid on the right, enlarging on a photocopier if needed, to sketch your growing space and identify sunny and shady areas.

Plot Shade and Sun

Watch your yard or growing space for a day, checking at regular intervals (such as once an hour), and note the areas that receive sun and shade. This will shift over the course of your growing season. Plant accordingly.

Diagram Your Space

Consider each plant's spacing needs before planting. Vining plants, such as cucumbers, will sprawl out and require trellising or a greater growing area than root crops like carrots. Be sure to avoid pairing plants that naturally compete or harm each other (see the Companion Planting Guide on page 258).

Also consider if your annual plants need to be rotated. Some herbs will reseed, some can be planted in the same place year after year, and some may need to be moved after depleting the soil of certain nutrients during the previous growing season.

Determine Your Last Spring Frost Date

Using data from the previous year, estimate the last spring frost date for your area and note what you'll need to plant before or after this date. Refer to seed packets, plant tags, and experts at your local garden center or university extension for the ideal planting time for each plant.

My 2023 last spring frost date: _____

Growing Space Grid

☐ = _____ feet

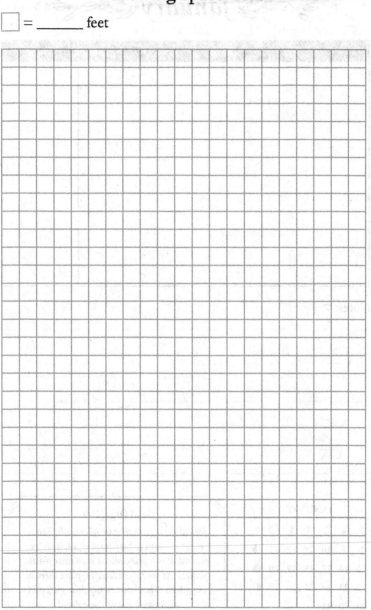

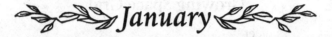

January

Task	Date

Notes:

_____

_____

_____

_____

_____

_____

_____

_____

JANUARY

1	2	3	4	5	○	7
8	9	10	11	12	13	◑
15	16	17	18	19	20	●
22	23	24	25	26	27	◐
29	30	31				

Seed Organizer

January is a great time to order seeds. Sometimes it's hard to keep track of what we've ordered. Buy a photo album with clear plastic pockets. As your seeds come in, place them in the album. Then you can flip through it and easily see what you've ordered.

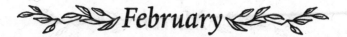

February

Task	Date

Notes:

_____

_____

_____

_____

_____

_____

_____

_____

Lawn Mower Care

Quiet February days are a good time to get your lawn mower ready for spring. Many lawn mower repair centers will pick up your mower. Have them check the oil, check the filter, sharpen the blade, and change the spark plug.

FEBRUARY

			1	2	3	4
○	6	7	8	9	10	11
12	◐	14	15	16	17	18
19	●	21	22	23	24	25
26	◑	28				

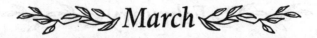

March

Task	Date

Notes:

_____

_____

_____

_____

_____

_____

_____

MARCH

			1	2	3	4
5	6	○	8	9	10	11
12	13	◑	15	16	17	18
19	20	●	22	23	24	25
26	27	◐	29	30	31	

Cool-Weather Planting

March is the perfect time to get some cool-weather plants started directly in the garden. These include onions, lettuce, and dill. For early-season color, plant pansies, violas, and primrose.

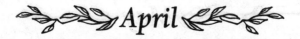
April

Task	Date

Notes:

_____

_____

_____

_____

_____

_____

_____

<table>
<tr><td>Root Health</td></tr>
<tr><td>When transplanting herbs and flowers from a pot to the garden, remember to "massage" the roots. To do this, remove the plant from the pot and gently spread out the roots, then place in the planting hole. This massage helps the plant get established more quickly.</td></tr>
</table>

APRIL

						1
2	3	4	5	○	7	8
9	10	11	12	◑	14	15
16	17	18	19	●	21	22
23	24	25	26	◐	28	29
30						

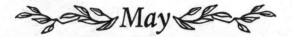

May

Task	Date

Notes:

_____

_____

_____

_____

_____

_____

_____

MAY

	1	2	3	4	○	6
7	8	9	10	11	◑	13
14	15	16	17	18	●	20
21	22	23	24	25	26	◐
28	29	30	31			

Planting Seeds before a Storm

When sowing seeds directly into the garden before an approaching thunderstorm, you should still water the seeds after planting. The watering will anchor the seeds in the soil, and when the heavy rain begins, the seeds won't be washed away.

June

Task	Date

Notes:

_____

_____

_____

_____

_____

_____

_____

_____

Fragrance in the Garden

To increase fragrance in your herb garden, plant low-growing fragrant herbs along the edge of the garden or along the garden's path. That way you'll brush them as you walk past and release their scent.

JUNE

				1	2	○
4	5	6	7	8	9	◑
11	12	13	14	15	16	17
●	19	20	21	22	23	24
25	◐	27	28	29	30	

July

Task	Date

Notes:

_____

_____

_____

_____

_____

_____

_____

JULY

						1
2	○	4	5	6	7	8
◑	10	11	12	13	14	15
16	●	18	19	20	21	22
23	24	◐	26	27	28	29
30	31					

Fresh Floral Bouquets

To enjoy cut flowers longer in the home, follow these simple rules. Cut the stems from the plant; don't pull them. Remove foliage from the cut stem; this will keep the water fresher. Place cut flowers in a vase of cool water.

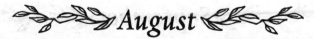

August

Task	Date

Notes:

_____

_____

_____

_____

_____

_____

_____

Peel Tomatoes Quickly

To peel tomatoes, try this: Fill a 3-quart saucepan with water and bring it to a boil. Drop 6–8 medium-size tomatoes into the boiling water. Turn off the heat. Leave the tomatoes in the water for 5 minutes. Rinse in cool water. The skins will slip off.

AUGUST

		○	2	3	4	5
6	7	◑	9	10	11	12
13	14	15	●	17	18	19
20	21	22	23	◐	25	26
27	28	29	○	31		

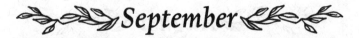

September

Task	Date

Notes:

_____

_____

_____

_____

_____

_____

_____

SEPTEMBER						
					1	2
3	4	5	◑	7	8	9
10	11	12	13	●	15	16
17	18	19	20	21	◐	23
24	25	26	27	28	○	30

Harvesting Basil

Harvest basil on a sunny morning when the herbal oils are strongest. Cut stems at the base of the plant and rinse in cool water. Dry well on paper towels. Tie 3–4 stems together. Hang in an airy place away from direct sun until completely dry.

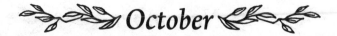

October

Task	Date

Notes:

_____

_____

_____

_____

_____

_____

_____

Wildflowers for Spring

October is a great time to plant wildflower seeds for next spring. Wait until you've had a few hard frosts—that way the seeds will remain dormant. Work the soil and plant the seeds according to the directions. Come next spring, your wildflowers will bloom earlier.

OCTOBER

1	2	3	4	5	◑	7
8	9	10	11	12	13	●
15	16	17	18	19	20	◐
22	23	24	25	26	27	○
29	30	31				

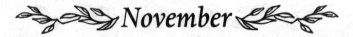

November

Task	Date

Notes:

_____

_____

_____

_____

_____

_____

_____

_____

NOVEMBER					
		1	2	3	4
◑ 6	7	8	9	10	11
12 ●	14	15	16	17	18
19 ◐	21	22	23	24	25
26 ○	28	29	30		

Garden Cleanup

To clean the herb garden in the fall, first remove any diseased or dead plants. Throw them away—never compost them. The disease may spread to other plants. Rake and compost most leaves. Allow some leaves to remain in the garden. They'll decay and add nutrients to the soil.

Task	Date

Notes:

_____

_____

_____

_____

_____

_____

_____

Clean Garden Tools

Time to clean your garden tools. Begin by removing any mud from all metal parts. When the metal is dry, sharpen if needed. End by putting a few drops of lubricating oil on a soft rag and rubbing the oil over blades, etc. Now, hang up your hoe and relax!

DECEMBER

					1	2
3	4	◑ 5	6	7	8	9
10	11	● 12	13	14	15	16
17	18	◐ 19	20	21	22	23
24	25	○ 26	27	28	29	30
31						

Gardening by the Moon

It is believed that the moon's gravitational pull extends beyond Earth's oceans, affecting the moisture in the soil, seeds, and plants. Some gardeners utilize this timing to strategically plan various gardening activities. Here's how:

Gardening by Moon Phase

During the waxing moon (from new moon to full moon), plant annuals, crops that need to be seeded anew each year, and those that produce their yield above the ground. During the waning moon (from full moon to new moon), plant biennials, perennials, and bulb and root plants. As a rule, these are plants that produce below the ground.

These are not hard and fast divisions. If you can't plant during the first quarter, plant during the second, and vice versa. There are many plants that seem to do equally well planted in either quarter, such as watermelon, hay, and cereals and grains.

First Quarter (Waxing): The first quarter begins with the new moon. Plant annuals that produce their yield above the ground and are generally of the leafy kind that produce their seed outside their fruit. Examples are asparagus, broccoli, brussels sprouts, cabbage, cauliflower, celery, cress, endive, kohlrabi, lettuce, parsley, and spinach. Cucumbers are an exception, as they do best in the first quarter rather than the second, even though the seeds are inside the fruit. Also in the first quarter, plant cereals and grains.

Second Quarter (Waxing): Plant annuals that produce their yield above ground and are generally the viney types that produce their seed inside the fruit. Examples include beans, eggplant, melons, peas, peppers, pumpkins, squash, and tomatoes.

Third Quarter (Waning): The third quarter begins with the full moon. Plant biennials, perennials, and bulb and root plants. Also plant trees, shrubs, berries, beets, carrots, onions, parsnips, peanuts, potatoes, radishes, rhubarb, rutabagas, strawberries, turnips, winter wheat, and grapes.

Fourth Quarter (Waning): This is the best time to cultivate, turn sod, pull weeds, and destroy pests of all kinds, especially when the moon is in the barren signs of Aries, Leo, Virgo, Gemini, Aquarius, and Sagittarius.

Gardening by Moon Sign

Some gardeners include the influence of the twelve astrological signs in their lunar gardening as well. The moon changes sign roughly every two and a half days.

Moon in Aries: Barren and dry. Used for destroying noxious growth, weeds, pests, and so on, and for cultivating.

Moon in Taurus: Productive and moist. Used for planting many crops, particularly potatoes and root crops, and when hardiness is important. Also used for lettuce, cabbage, and similar leafy vegetables.

Moon in Gemini: Barren and dry. Used for destroying noxious growths, weeds, and pests, and for cultivation.

Moon in Cancer: Very fruitful and moist. This is the most productive sign, used extensively for planting and irrigation.

Moon in Leo: Barren and dry. This is the most barren sign, used only for killing weeds and for cultivation.

Moon in Virgo: Barren and moist. Good for cultivation and destroying weeds and pests.

Moon in Libra: Semi-fruitful and moist. Used for planting many crops and producing good pulp growth and roots. A very good sign for flowers and vines. Also used for seeding hay, corn fodder, etc.

Moon in Scorpio: Very fruitful and moist. Nearly as productive as Cancer; used for the same purposes. Especially good for vine growth and sturdiness.

Moon in Sagittarius: Barren and dry. Used for planting onions, for seeding hay, and for cultivation.

Moon in Capricorn: Productive and dry. Used for planting potatoes, tubers, etc.

Moon in Aquarius: Barren and dry. Used for cultivation and destroying noxious growths, weeds, and pests.

Moon in Pisces: Very fruitful and moist. Used along with Cancer and Scorpio, and especially good for root growth.

Planting Guide for Moon Phase and Sign

The following table shows how to combine the moon's quarters and signs to choose the best planting dates for crops, flowers, and trees.

Plant	Quarter	Sign
Annuals	1st or 2nd	*See specific entry*
Apple trees	2nd or 3rd	Cancer, Pisces, Taurus
Asparagus	1st	Cancer, Scorpio, Pisces
Barley	1st or 2nd	Cancer, Pisces, Libra, Capricorn
Beans	2nd	Cancer, Pisces, Libra, Taurus
Beets	3rd	Cancer, Pisces, Libra, Capricorn
Berries	2nd	Cancer, Scorpio, Pisces
Biennials	3rd or 4th	*See specific entry*
Broccoli	1st	Cancer, Scorpio, Pisces, Libra
Brussels sprouts	1st	Cancer, Scorpio, Pisces, Libra

Plant	Quarter	Sign
Buckwheat	1st or 2nd	Capricorn
Bulbs	3rd	Cancer, Scorpio, Pisces
Bulbs for seed	2nd or 3rd	*See specific entry*
Cabbage	1st	Cancer, Scorpio, Pisces, Taurus
Cantaloupes	1st or 2nd	Cancer, Scorpio, Pisces, Taurus
Carrots	3rd	Cancer, Scorpio, Pisces, Libra
Cauliflower	1st	Cancer, Scorpio, Pisces, Libra
Celery	1st	Cancer, Scorpio, Pisces
Cereals	1st or 2nd	Cancer, Scorpio, Pisces, Libra
Chard	1st or 2nd	Cancer, Scorpio, Pisces
Chicory	2nd or 3rd	Cancer, Scorpio, Pisces
Clover	1st or 2nd	Cancer, Scorpio, Pisces
Corn	1st	Cancer, Scorpio, Pisces
Corn for fodder	1st or 2nd	Libra
Cress	1st	Cancer, Scorpio, Pisces
Cucumbers	1st	Cancer, Scorpio, Pisces
Deciduous trees	2nd or 3rd	Cancer, Scorpio, Pisces, Virgo
Eggplant	2nd	Cancer, Scorpio, Pisces, Libra
Endive	1st	Cancer, Scorpio, Pisces, Libra
Flowers	1st	Taurus, Virgo, Cancer, Scorpio, Pisces, Libra
Garlic	3rd	Libra, Taurus, Pisces
Gourds	1st or 2nd	Cancer, Scorpio, Pisces, Libra
Melons	2nd	Cancer, Scorpio, Pisces
Onion seeds	2nd	Scorpio, Cancer, Sagittarius
Onion sets	3rd or 4th	Libra, Taurus, Pisces, Cancer
Parsley	1st	Cancer, Scorpio, Pisces, Libra
Parsnips	3rd	Cancer, Scorpio, Pisces, Taurus
Peach trees	2nd or 3rd	Taurus, Libra, Virgo

Plant	Quarter	Sign
Peanuts	3rd	Cancer, Scorpio, Pisces
Pear trees	2nd or 3rd	Taurus, Libra, Virgo
Perennials	3rd	*See specific entry*
Plum trees	2nd or 3rd	Taurus, Libra, Virgo
Pole beans	1st or 2nd	Scorpio
Potatoes	3rd	Cancer, Scorpio, Taurus, Libra
Pumpkins	2nd	Cancer, Scorpio, Pisces, Libra
Quinces	1st or 2nd	Capricorn
Radishes	3rd	Libra, Taurus, Pisces, Capricorn
Rice	1st or 2nd	Scorpio
Roses	1st or 2nd	Cancer
Rutabagas	3rd	Cancer, Scorpio, Pisces, Taurus
Sage	3rd	Cancer, Scorpio, Pisces
Salsify	1st or 2nd	Cancer, Scorpio, Pisces
Spinach	1st	Cancer, Scorpio, Pisces
Squash	2nd	Cancer, Scorpio, Taurus, Libra
Strawberries	3rd	Cancer, Scorpio, Pisces
String beans	1st or 2nd	Taurus
Sunflowers	2nd, 3rd, 4th	Cancer, Libra
Tomatoes	2nd	Cancer, Scorpio, Pisces, Capricorn
Tulips	1st or 2nd	Libra, Virgo
Turnips	3rd	Cancer, Scorpio, Pisces, Taurus
Watermelon	1st or 2nd	Cancer, Scorpio, Pisces, Libra

2023 Moon Signs and Phases

Cross-reference the following month-by-month tables with the planting guide for moon phase and sign to determine the recommended planting times for 2023. Gray rows indicate the day of a phase change. All times are in Eastern Standard and Eastern Daylight Time, so be sure to adjust for your time zone.

January 2023

Date	Sign	Phase
1 Sun	Taurus	2nd
2 Mon 9:44 pm	Gemini	2nd
3 Tue	Gemini	2nd
4 Wed	Gemini	2nd
5 Thu 9:15 am	Cancer	2nd
6 Fri	Cancer	Full 6:08 pm
7 Sat 9:40 pm	Leo	3rd
8 Sun	Leo	3rd
9 Mon	Leo	3rd
10 Tue 10:15 am	Virgo	3rd
11 Wed	Virgo	3rd
12 Thu 9:56 pm	Libra	3rd
13 Fri	Libra	3rd
14 Sat	Libra	4th 9:10 pm
15 Sun 7:08 am	Scorpio	4th
16 Mon	Scorpio	4th
17 Tue 12:33 pm	Sagittarius	4th
18 Wed	Sagittarius	4th
19 Thu 2:11 pm	Capricorn	4th
20 Fri	Capricorn	4th
21 Sat 1:29 pm	Aquarius	New 3:53 pm
22 Sun	Aquarius	1st
23 Mon 12:36 pm	Pisces	1st
24 Tue	Pisces	1st
25 Wed 1:48 pm	Aries	1st
26 Thu	Aries	1st
27 Fri 6:42 pm	Taurus	1st
28 Sat	Taurus	2nd 10:19 am
29 Sun	Taurus	2nd
30 Mon 3:35 am	Gemini	2nd
31 Tue	Gemini	2nd

February 2023

Date	Sign	Phase
1 Wed 3:11 pm	Cancer	2nd
2 Thu	Cancer	2nd
3 Fri	Cancer	2nd
4 Sat 3:48 am	Leo	2nd
5 Sun	Leo	Full 1:29 pm
6 Mon 4:14 pm	Virgo	3rd
7 Tue	Virgo	3rd
8 Wed	Virgo	3rd
9 Thu 3:47 am	Libra	3rd
10 Fri	Libra	3rd
11 Sat 1:34 pm	Scorpio	3rd
12 Sun	Scorpio	3rd
13 Mon 8:31 pm	Sagittarius	4th 11:01 am
14 Tue	Sagittarius	4th
15 Wed	Sagittarius	4th
16 Thu 12:00 am	Capricorn	4th
17 Fri	Capricorn	4th
18 Sat 12:35 am	Aquarius	4th
19 Sun 11:56 pm	Pisces	4th
20 Mon	Pisces	New 2:06 am
21 Tue	Pisces	1st
22 Wed 12:14 am	Aries	1st
23 Thu	Aries	1st
24 Fri 3:29 am	Taurus	1st
25 Sat	Taurus	1st
26 Sun 10:48 am	Gemini	1st
27 Mon	Gemini	2nd 3:06 am
28 Tue 9:40 pm	Cancer	2nd

March 2023

Date	Sign	Phase
1 Wed	Cancer	2nd
2 Thu	Cancer	2nd
3 Fri 10:16 am	Leo	2nd
4 Sat	Leo	2nd
5 Sun 10:38 pm	Virgo	2nd
6 Mon	Virgo	2nd
7 Tue	Virgo	Full 7:40 am
8 Wed 9:44 am	Libra	3rd
9 Thu	Libra	3rd
10 Fri 7:06 pm	Scorpio	3rd
11 Sat	Scorpio	3rd
12 Sun	Scorpio	3rd
13 Mon 3:21 am	Sagittarius	3rd
14 Tue	Sagittarius	4th 10:08 pm
15 Wed 8:06 am	Capricorn	4th
16 Thu	Capricorn	4th
17 Fri 10:25 am	Aquarius	4th
18 Sat	Aquarius	4th
19 Sun 11:12 am	Pisces	4th
20 Mon	Pisces	4th
21 Tue 12:01 pm	Aries	New 1:23 pm
22 Wed	Aries	1st
23 Thu 2:42 pm	Taurus	1st
24 Fri	Taurus	1st
25 Sat 8:42 pm	Gemini	1st
26 Sun	Gemini	1st
27 Mon	Gemini	1st
28 Tue 6:22 am	Cancer	2nd 10:32 pm
29 Wed	Cancer	2nd
30 Thu 6:31 pm	Leo	2nd
31 Fri	Leo	2nd

April 2023

Date	Sign	Phase
1 Sat	Leo	2nd
2 Sun 6:57 am	Virgo	2nd
3 Mon	Virgo	2nd
4 Tue 5:51 pm	Libra	2nd
5 Wed	Libra	2nd
6 Thu	Libra	Full 12:34 am
7 Fri 2:29 am	Scorpio	3rd
8 Sat	Scorpio	3rd
9 Sun 8:57 am	Sagittarius	3rd
10 Mon	Sagittarius	3rd
11 Tue 1:33 pm	Capricorn	3rd
12 Wed	Capricorn	3rd
13 Thu 4:42 pm	Aquarius	4th 5:11 am
14 Fri	Aquarius	4th
15 Sat 6:57 pm	Pisces	4th
16 Sun	Pisces	4th
17 Mon 9:09 pm	Aries	4th
18 Tue	Aries	4th
19 Wed	Aries	4th
20 Thu 12:30 am	Taurus	New 12:13 am
21 Fri	Taurus	1st
22 Sat 6:11 am	Gemini	1st
23 Sun	Gemini	1st
24 Mon 2:58 pm	Cancer	1st
25 Tue	Cancer	1st
26 Wed	Cancer	1st
27 Thu 2:30 am	Leo	2nd 5:20 pm
28 Fri	Leo	2nd
29 Sat 2:59 pm	Virgo	2nd
30 Sun	Virgo	2nd

May 2023

Date	Sign	Phase
1 Mon	Virgo	2nd
2 Tue 2:09 am	Libra	2nd
3 Wed	Libra	2nd
4 Thu 10:32 am	Scorpio	2nd
5 Fri	Scorpio	Full 1:34 pm
6 Sat 4:04 pm	Sagittarius	3rd
7 Sun	Sagittarius	3rd
8 Mon 7:33 pm	Capricorn	3rd
9 Tue	Capricorn	3rd
10 Wed 10:05 pm	Aquarius	3rd
11 Thu	Aquarius	3rd
12 Fri	Aquarius	4th 10:28 am
13 Sat 12:39 am	Pisces	4th
14 Sun	Pisces	4th
15 Mon 3:56 am	Aries	4th
16 Tue	Aries	4th
17 Wed 8:28 am	Taurus	4th
18 Thu	Taurus	4th
19 Fri 2:48 pm	Gemini	New 11:53 am
20 Sat	Gemini	1st
21 Sun 11:28 pm	Cancer	1st
22 Mon	Cancer	1st
23 Tue	Cancer	1st
24 Wed 10:35 am	Leo	1st
25 Thu	Leo	1st
26 Fri 11:05 pm	Virgo	1st
27 Sat	Virgo	2nd 11:22 am
28 Sun	Virgo	2nd
29 Mon 10:51 am	Libra	2nd
30 Tue	Libra	2nd
31 Wed 7:45 pm	Scorpio	2nd

June 2023

Date	Sign	Phase
1 Thu	Scorpio	2nd
2 Fri	Scorpio	2nd
3 Sat 1:03 am	Sagittarius	Full 11:42 pm
4 Sun	Sagittarius	3rd
5 Mon 3:31 am	Capricorn	3rd
6 Tue	Capricorn	3rd
7 Wed 4:42 am	Aquarius	3rd
8 Thu	Aquarius	3rd
9 Fri 6:14 am	Pisces	3rd
10 Sat	Pisces	4th 3:31 pm
11 Sun 9:20 am	Aries	4th
12 Mon	Aries	4th
13 Tue 2:31 pm	Taurus	4th
14 Wed	Taurus	4th
15 Thu 9:46 pm	Gemini	4th
16 Fri	Gemini	4th
17 Sat	Gemini	4th
18 Sun 6:58 am	Cancer	New 12:37 am
19 Mon	Cancer	1st
20 Tue 6:04 pm	Leo	1st
21 Wed	Leo	1st
22 Thu	Leo	1st
23 Fri 6:35 am	Virgo	1st
24 Sat	Virgo	1st
25 Sun 6:57 pm	Libra	1st
26 Mon	Libra	2nd 3:50 am
27 Tue	Libra	2nd
28 Wed 4:55 am	Scorpio	2nd
29 Thu	Scorpio	2nd
30 Fri 10:59 am	Sagittarius	2nd

July 2023

Date	Sign	Phase
1 Sat	Sagittarius	2nd
2 Sun 1:20 pm	Capricorn	2nd
3 Mon	Capricorn	Full 7:39 am
4 Tue 1:30 pm	Aquarius	3rd
5 Wed	Aquarius	3rd
6 Thu 1:33 pm	Pisces	3rd
7 Fri	Pisces	3rd
8 Sat 3:19 pm	Aries	3rd
9 Sun	Aries	4th 9:48 pm
10 Mon 7:55 pm	Taurus	4th
11 Tue	Taurus	4th
12 Wed	Taurus	4th
13 Thu 3:26 am	Gemini	4th
14 Fri	Gemini	4th
15 Sat 1:13 pm	Cancer	4th
16 Sun	Cancer	4th
17 Mon	Cancer	New 2:32 pm
18 Tue 12:39 am	Leo	1st
19 Wed	Leo	1st
20 Thu 1:13 pm	Virgo	1st
21 Fri	Virgo	1st
22 Sat	Virgo	1st
23 Sun 1:54 am	Libra	1st
24 Mon	Libra	1st
25 Tue 12:55 pm	Scorpio	2nd 6:07 pm
26 Wed	Scorpio	2nd
27 Thu 8:24 pm	Sagittarius	2nd
28 Fri	Sagittarius	2nd
29 Sat 11:44 pm	Capricorn	2nd
30 Sun	Capricorn	2nd
31 Mon 11:58 pm	Aquarius	2nd

August 2023

1 Tue	Aquarius	Full 2:32 pm
2 Wed 11:05 pm	Pisces	3rd
3 Thu	Pisces	3rd
4 Fri 11:19 pm	Aries	3rd
5 Sat	Aries	3rd
6 Sun	Aries	3rd
7 Mon 2:25 am	Taurus	3rd
8 Tue	Taurus	4th 6:28 am
9 Wed 9:05 am	Gemini	4th
10 Thu	Gemini	4th
11 Fri 6:52 pm	Cancer	4th
12 Sat	Cancer	4th
13 Sun	Cancer	4th
14 Mon 6:36 am	Leo	4th
15 Tue	Leo	4th
16 Wed 7:14 pm	Virgo	New 5:38 am
17 Thu	Virgo	1st
18 Fri	Virgo	1st
19 Sat 7:53 am	Libra	1st
20 Sun	Libra	1st
21 Mon 7:22 pm	Scorpio	1st
22 Tue	Scorpio	1st
23 Wed	Scorpio	1st
24 Thu 4:07 am	Sagittarius	2nd 5:57 am
25 Fri	Sagittarius	2nd
26 Sat 9:05 am	Capricorn	2nd
27 Sun	Capricorn	2nd
28 Mon 10:32 am	Aquarius	2nd
29 Tue	Aquarius	2nd
30 Wed 9:56 am	Pisces	Full 9:36 pm
31 Thu	Pisces	3rd

September 2023

Date	Sign	Phase
1 Fri 9:25 am	Aries	3rd
2 Sat	Aries	3rd
3 Sun 11:00 am	Taurus	3rd
4 Mon	Taurus	3rd
5 Tue 4:07 pm	Gemini	3rd
6 Wed	Gemini	4th 6:21 pm
7 Thu	Gemini	4th
8 Fri 1:00 am	Cancer	4th
9 Sat	Cancer	4th
10 Sun 12:36 pm	Leo	4th
11 Mon	Leo	4th
12 Tue	Leo	4th
13 Wed 1:18 am	Virgo	4th
14 Thu	Virgo	New 9:40 pm
15 Fri 1:44 pm	Libra	1st
16 Sat	Libra	1st
17 Sun	Libra	1st
18 Mon 12:58 am	Scorpio	1st
19 Tue	Scorpio	1st
20 Wed 10:06 am	Sagittarius	1st
21 Thu	Sagittarius	1st
22 Fri 4:20 pm	Capricorn	2nd 3:32 pm
23 Sat	Capricorn	2nd
24 Sun 7:29 pm	Aquarius	2nd
25 Mon	Aquarius	2nd
26 Tue 8:18 pm	Pisces	2nd
27 Wed	Pisces	2nd
28 Thu 8:17 pm	Aries	2nd
29 Fri	Aries	Full 5:58 am
30 Sat 9:18 pm	Taurus	3rd

October 2023

Date	Sign	Phase
1 Sun	Taurus	3rd
2 Mon	Taurus	3rd
3 Tue 1:03 am	Gemini	3rd
4 Wed	Gemini	3rd
5 Thu 8:32 am	Cancer	3rd
6 Fri	Cancer	4th 9:48 am
7 Sat 7:24 pm	Leo	4th
8 Sun	Leo	4th
9 Mon	Leo	4th
10 Tue 8:02 am	Virgo	4th
11 Wed	Virgo	4th
12 Thu 8:22 pm	Libra	4th
13 Fri	Libra	4th
14 Sat	Libra	New 1:55 pm
15 Sun 7:04 am	Scorpio	1st
16 Mon	Scorpio	1st
17 Tue 3:36 pm	Sagittarius	1st
18 Wed	Sagittarius	1st
19 Thu 9:55 pm	Capricorn	1st
20 Fri	Capricorn	1st
21 Sat	Capricorn	2nd 11:29 pm
22 Sun 2:06 am	Aquarius	2nd
23 Mon	Aquarius	2nd
24 Tue 4:33 am	Pisces	2nd
25 Wed	Pisces	2nd
26 Thu 6:02 am	Aries	2nd
27 Fri	Aries	2nd
28 Sat 7:44 am	Taurus	Full 4:24 pm
29 Sun	Taurus	3rd
30 Mon 11:08 am	Gemini	3rd
31 Tue	Gemini	3rd

November 2023

Date	Sign	Phase
1 Wed 5:30 pm	Cancer	3rd
2 Thu	Cancer	3rd
3 Fri	Cancer	3rd
4 Sat 3:21 am	Leo	3rd
5 Sun	Leo	4th 3:37 am
6 Mon 2:39 pm	Virgo	4th
7 Tue	Virgo	4th
8 Wed	Virgo	4th
9 Thu 3:08 am	Libra	4th
10 Fri	Libra	4th
11 Sat 1:39 pm	Scorpio	4th
12 Sun	Scorpio	4th
13 Mon 9:23 pm	Sagittarius	New 4:27 am
14 Tue	Sagittarius	1st
15 Wed	Sagittarius	1st
16 Thu 2:41 am	Capricorn	1st
17 Fri	Capricorn	1st
18 Sat 6:28 am	Aquarius	1st
19 Sun	Aquarius	1st
20 Mon 9:29 am	Pisces	2nd 5:50 am
21 Tue	Pisces	2nd
22 Wed 12:19 pm	Aries	2nd
23 Thu	Aries	2nd
24 Fri 3:29 pm	Taurus	2nd
25 Sat	Taurus	2nd
26 Sun 7:40 pm	Gemini	2nd
27 Mon	Gemini	Full 4:16 am
28 Tue	Gemini	3rd
29 Wed 1:54 am	Cancer	3rd
30 Thu	Cancer	3rd

December 2023

Date	Sign	Phase
1 Fri 11:00 am	Leo	3rd
2 Sat	Leo	3rd
3 Sun 10:50 pm	Virgo	3rd
4 Mon	Virgo	3rd
5 Tue	Virgo	4th 12:49 am
6 Wed 11:35 am	Libra	4th
7 Thu	Libra	4th
8 Fri 10:35 pm	Scorpio	4th
9 Sat	Scorpio	4th
10 Sun	Scorpio	4th
11 Mon 6:11 am	Sagittarius	4th
12 Tue	Sagittarius	New 6:32 pm
13 Wed 10:31 am	Capricorn	1st
14 Thu	Capricorn	1st
15 Fri 12:56 pm	Aquarius	1st
16 Sat	Aquarius	1st
17 Sun 2:58 pm	Pisces	1st
18 Mon	Pisces	1st
19 Tue 5:47 pm	Aries	2nd 1:39 pm
20 Wed	Aries	2nd
21 Thu 9:50 pm	Taurus	2nd
22 Fri	Taurus	2nd
23 Sat	Taurus	2nd
24 Sun 3:15 am	Gemini	2nd
25 Mon	Gemini	2nd
26 Tue 10:15 am	Cancer	Full 7:33 pm
27 Wed	Cancer	3rd
28 Thu 7:23 pm	Leo	3rd
29 Fri	Leo	3rd
30 Sat	Leo	3rd
31 Sat 12:08 pm	Taurus	2nd

Contributors

Anne Sala is a freelance writer located in Minnesota. She writes, gardens, and cooks alongside her two children and husband, who are usually eager to help. She has been a regular contributor to Llewellyn's annuals for more than fifteen years.

Annie Burdick is a writer and editor living in Portland, Oregon. She has written for numerous websites, magazines, and anthologies on wildly varied topics. She is also the author of *Unconscious Bias*, *Bring the Wild Into Your Garden*, and *Gardening for Mind, Body, and Soul*, published by an imprint of Hachette UK. She spends most of her spare time reading, playing with her rescue dogs, and having adventures around the Pacific Northwest. Find her at annieburdickfreelance.com.

Autumn Damiana is an author, artist, crafter, amateur photographer, and regular contributor to Llewellyn's annuals. Along with writing and making art, Autumn has a degree in early childhood education. She lives with her husband and doggy familiar in the beautiful San Francisco Bay Area. Visit her online at autumndamiana.com.

Charlie Rainbow Wolf is happiest when she is creating something, especially if it's made from items that others have discarded. A recorded singer-songwriter and published author, she champions holistic living and lives in the Midwest with her husband and special-needs Great Danes. Astrology reports, smudge pots, smudge blends, and more are available through her website at charlierainbow.com.

Dawn Ritchie is an author, journalist, multimedia content provider, and TV writer/producer. Her work has appeared on all major networks, and her articles on design, cuisine, health, business, and entertainment have been published in dozens of national newspapers and publications. A contributor to the 2019, 2020, and 2022 editions of the *Herbal Almanac*, Dawn is also an avid organic gardener, forager, cook, passionate beekeeper, and author of *The Emotional House* (New Harbinger Publications).

Diana Rajchel is the author of *Urban Magick: A Guide for the City Witch* and *Hex Twisting: Counter Magick Spells for the Irritated Witch*. She splits geographic time between San Francisco, where she co-owns Golden Apple Metaphysical with her business partner Nikki, and Kalamazoo, Michigan, where she writes, teaches, reads tarot, and community-builds with her romantic partner Synty and their children. She is about eight years behind in her sleep but hopes to catch up someday.

Elizabeth Barrette lives in central Illinois and enjoys magical crafts, historic religions, and gardening for wildlife. She has written columns on Pagan practice, speculative fiction, gender studies, and social and environmental issues. Her book *Composing Magic* explains how to combine writing and spirituality. Visit her blog at ysabetwordsmith.dreamwidth.org.

This is **James Kambos**'s twenty-fifth year writing for Llewellyn Publications. He has written many articles about folk magic traditions, spellcraft, and herbs. He's also an artist and has designed cards and calendars. A gardener, he raises a large variety of herbs and wildflowers. He lives in the beautiful Appalachian hill country of Southern Ohio.

Janesh Vaidya (Kerala, India) was born into a family of traditional Ayurveda practitioners in Kerala, South India. He has spent his life practicing and teaching Ayurveda in India, Europe, and the United States. His books have sold more than 130,000 copies in Sweden and have been translated into German, Dutch, Norwegian, and Finnish.

JD Walker resides in North Carolina. She is an avid student of herbology and gardening. She has written a weekly garden column since 1991. She is an award-winning author, journalist, and magazine editor and a frequent contributor to the Llewellyn annuals. Her book, *A Witch's Guide to Wildcraft*, was published by Llewellyn Publications in 2021. When not at the keyboard, she spends time in her own landscape, taking trips with friends, and with her nose buried in a book.

Jill Henderson is a backwoods herbalist, author, artist, and world traveler with a penchant for wild edible and medicinal plants, culinary herbs, and nature ecology. She is a longtime contributor to *Llewellyn's Herbal Almanac* and *Acres USA* magazine and is the author of *The Healing Power of Kitchen Herbs, A Journey of Seasons*, and *The Garden Seed Saving Guide*. Visit Jill's blog at ShowMeOz.wordpress.com.

Jordan Charbonneau is a homesteader, hiker, animal lover, and forager. She attended Sterling College (Vermont), where she double majored in ecology and environmental humanities. Today, Jordan lives in a little off-grid cabin she and her husband Scott built in the hills of West Virginia. Together they grow organic vegetables and care for tons of animals. You can find more of her writing at rabbitridgefarmwv.com.

Kathy Keeler grew up in New York and Ohio, attended the University of Michigan, and received her PhD in genetics from the University of California, Berkeley. She was a professor of plant ecology in the School of Biological Sciences at the University of Nebraska-Lincoln for thirty-one years. In retirement, she traveled. Still excited about plants, she became *A Wandering Botanist*, blogging and speaking about plants, travel, and history. She lives in Colorado with her husband, two cats, and many intriguing plants.

Kathy Martin is the longtime author of the blog *Skippy's Vegetable Garden*, a journal of her vegetable gardens, which has won awards including *Horticulture Magazine*'s Best Gardening Blog. She recently founded Aurelia's Garden Inc., a microfarm that grows vegetables for local food pantries. Kathy writes gardening apps and is a certified Master Gardener. She is a retired biomedical researcher who lives near Boston with her family, dogs, chickens, and honeybees.

Linda Raedisch is a writer, papercrafter, suburban explorer, and general mucker-about in the kitchen. Her most recent book for Llewellyn is *The Lore of Old Elfland: Secrets from the Bronze Age to Middle Earth*. To see what she's up to, follow her on Instagram at @lindaraedisch.

Lupa is a naturalist Pagan author and artist in the Pacific Northwest. She is the author of several books on nature-based Paganism, including *Nature Spirituality From the Ground Up: Connect With Totems in Your Ecosystem* and *The Tarot of Bones* deck and book. More about Lupa and her works may be found at thegreenwolf.com.

Marilyn I. Bellemore is an elementary school teacher, an editor, and the author of two traditionally published nonfiction books. She moved back to her native Rhode Island in summer 2021 after living in rural central Vermont for four years. Fortunately, she resides in an old Victorian house by the ocean, where the yard is landscaped with abundant flower and vegetable gardens and she has all the herbs and vegetables she needs at her fingertips. She is looking forward to restoring her seaside home in East Point, Prince Edward Island.

Melissa Tipton is a Jungian Witch, Structural Integrator, and founder of the Real Magic Mystery School, where she teaches online courses in Jungian Magic, a potent blend of ancient magical techniques and modern psychological insights. She's the author of *Living Reiki: Heal Yourself and Transform Your Life* and *Llewellyn's Complete Book of Reiki*. Learn more and take a free class at www.realmagic.school.

Mireille Blacke, MA, LADC, RD, CD-N, is a licensed alcohol and drug counselor, registered dietitian, and freelance health and nutrition writer from the Hartford, Connecticut, area. She has written numerous articles for Llewellyn's annuals since 2014. Mireille worked in rock radio for two decades before shifting her career focus to media psychology, behavioral health nutrition, and addiction counseling. Her Bengal cats consume most of her free time and sanity.

Monica Crosson is the author of *Wild Magical Soul*, *The Magickal Family,* and *Summer Sage*. She is a Master Gardener who lives in the beautiful Pacific Northwest, happily digging in the dirt and tending her raspberries with her family and their small menagerie of farm animals. Monica is a regular contributor to Llewellyn's annuals as well as *Enchanted Living Magazine* and *Witchology Magazine*.

Natalie Zaman is the author of *Color and Conjure* and *Magical Destinations of the Northeast*. A regular contributor to various Llewellyn annual publications, she also writes the recurring feature Wandering Witch for *Witches & Pagans* magazine. When not on the road, she's busy tending her magical back garden. Visit Natalie online at nataliezaman.blogspot.com.

Rachael Witt is a community herbalist, gardener, and ancestral skills teacher. She is the founder of Wildness Within, an herbal business that offers plant-based classes and workshops, handmade products, and herbal consultations. Rachael is dedicated to simple, seasonal living with the land and teaching people hands-on earth skills. She lives and stewards the Highlands Homestead in Duvall, WA. Find more at www.Wildness WithinLiving.com

Susan Pesznecker is a mother, writer, nurse, and college English professor living in the beautiful Pacific Northwest with her poodles. An amateur herbalist, Sue loves reading, writing, cooking, travel, and anything having to do with the outdoors. Previous works include *Crafting Magick with Pen and Ink*, *The Magickal Retreat*, and *Yule: Recipes & Lore for the Winter Solstice*. She's a regular contributor to the Llewellyn annuals. Follow her on Instagram at @SusanPesznecker.

Suzanne Ress runs a small farm in the Alpine foothills of Italy, where she lives with her husband. She has been a practicing Pagan for as long as she can remember and was recently featured in the exhibit "Worldwide Witches" at the Hexenmuseum of Switzerland. She is the author of *The Trial of Goody Gilbert*.

Gardening Resources

Cooking with Herbs and Spices compiled by **Susan Pesznecker**
Gardening Techniques written by **Jill Henderson**
2023 Themed Garden Plans designed by **JD Walker**
2023 Gardening Log tips written by **James Kambos**